The Elixir Engineer

A Comprehensive Guide to Backend Development

Zion Edwin

Table of Contents

Preface

Hey there, fellow coder! Ever felt like you're hitting a wall with your backend development? Maybe you're tired of wrestling with concurrency, or you're craving that sweet feeling of building something truly robust and scalable. Well, you've come to the right place. This book is your friendly guide to becoming an Elixir Engineer, and trust me, it's going to be an exciting ride (without the rollercoaster nausea, thankfully!).

Background and Motivation

Let's be honest, the world of backend development is constantly evolving. New languages, frameworks, and tools pop up every day. So why Elixir? What makes it so special? For me, it was the "aha!" moment when I realized how effortlessly Elixir handles concurrency and fault-tolerance. Suddenly, building applications that could handle massive traffic and recover gracefully from errors felt not just possible, but actually enjoyable! I wrote this book because I want to share that excitement and empower you to build amazing things with Elixir.

Purpose and Scope

This book is your one-stop shop for mastering Elixir backend development. We'll start with the basics, laying a solid foundation in the language and its functional paradigm. Then, we'll ramp up to building real-world applications with Phoenix, Ecto, and OTP. By the end, you'll be equipped to tackle everything from APIs and real-time features to microservices and production deployments.

Think of this book as your trusty toolbox, packed with practical techniques, clear explanations, and real-world examples. No fluff, no jargon-filled lectures, just straightforward guidance to help you become a confident Elixir engineer.

Target Audience

This book is perfect for you if:

- You're a backend developer looking to explore a new language and expand your skillset.
- You're intrigued by Elixir and want a comprehensive guide to learn it effectively.
- You're already familiar with Elixir but want to deepen your understanding and build more sophisticated applications.
- You're passionate about creating scalable, maintainable, and fault-tolerant systems.

Whether you're a seasoned developer or just starting your coding adventure, this book will meet you where you are and guide you towards Elixir mastery.

Organization and Structure

This book is organized into three parts:

- **Part 1: Foundations:** We'll cover the essentials of Elixir, from syntax and data types to functional programming concepts and OTP basics.
- **Part 2: Backend Development with Elixir:** This is where the fun begins! You'll learn how to build web applications with Phoenix, interact with databases

using Ecto, and create real-time features with Phoenix Channels.

- **Part 3: Advanced Elixir Engineering:** We'll explore advanced topics like concurrency, distribution, debugging, performance tuning, and microservices.

Each chapter builds upon the previous one, providing a clear and logical progression. Code examples and practical exercises are sprinkled throughout to reinforce your learning and help you apply the concepts in real-world scenarios.

Invitation to Read

So, are you ready to unlock the power of Elixir and transform your approach to backend development? Grab a cup of coffee (or your beverage of choice), get comfortable, and let's embark on this exciting adventure together. I can't wait to see what you build!

Chapter 1: Welcome to Elixir!

Let's kick things off! You've cracked open this book, you're eager to learn Elixir, and I'm stoked to be your guide. In this chapter, we'll lay the groundwork for your Elixir journey. We'll explore why Elixir is such a fantastic choice for backend development, set up your coding environment, get a taste of the language's syntax, and even take Elixir's interactive shell for a spin.

1.1 Why Elixir?

You might be wondering, "Why Elixir? What makes this language stand out in the crowded field of backend development?" It's a great question, and the answer lies in a combination of powerful features and a unique approach to building software. Let's explore the key reasons why Elixir is gaining traction and becoming a popular choice for developers:

1. Concurrency:

Imagine your application as a bustling coffee shop. Multiple customers (requests) come in simultaneously, and you need to serve them all efficiently without making anyone wait too long. This is where concurrency comes in. Elixir, built on the Erlang Virtual Machine (BEAM), excels at handling many tasks concurrently.

Think of the BEAM as a highly organized team of baristas, each capable of handling a customer's order independently.

This allows your application to process numerous requests simultaneously, leading to faster response times and a smoother user experience, even under heavy load.

2. Fault-Tolerance:

Even the best coffee shops experience the occasional spilled latte or broken espresso machine. Similarly, software can encounter errors and unexpected situations. Elixir embraces this reality with its "let it crash" philosophy. Instead of trying to prevent every possible error, Elixir provides mechanisms to isolate and recover from failures gracefully.

Imagine each barista having their own designated workspace. If one barista makes a mistake, it doesn't affect the others. The faulty process can be restarted quickly, ensuring the coffee shop as a whole continues to operate smoothly. This approach makes Elixir applications incredibly resilient and reliable.

3. Functional Programming:

Elixir is a functional programming language. This means it emphasizes working with immutable data and composing functions to build logic. Think of it like assembling a complex LEGO creation from smaller, reusable bricks. Each function performs a specific task, and you combine them to achieve the desired outcome.

Immutability means that once a data structure is created, it cannot be changed. Instead of modifying existing data, you create new data structures with the desired changes. This might seem counterintuitive at first, but it leads to code that is easier to reason about, test, and maintain. It also eliminates many common sources of bugs related to data mutation.

4. Developer Experience:

Elixir's syntax is designed to be clear, concise, and readable. It draws inspiration from Ruby, known for its developer-friendly nature, while incorporating functional programming concepts. This results in a language that is both powerful and enjoyable to work with.

Elixir also provides excellent tooling, including an interactive shell called IEx (Interactive Elixir) that allows you to experiment with code and explore the language in a REPL (Read-Eval-Print Loop) environment. The community is active and supportive, offering ample resources and libraries to help you on your Elixir journey.

5. Ecosystem and Community:

Elixir has a thriving ecosystem with a growing collection of libraries and frameworks. Phoenix, a popular web framework built on Elixir, provides a productive and enjoyable way to build web applications. Ecto, a database wrapper and query language, simplifies database interactions.

The Elixir community is known for its welcoming and inclusive atmosphere. You'll find numerous online forums, conferences, and local meetups where you can connect with fellow Elixir enthusiasts, ask questions, and share knowledge.

In essence, Elixir offers a compelling blend of concurrency, fault-tolerance, functional programming, and developer-friendly features. This combination makes it an excellent choice for building a wide range of applications, from high-traffic web applications and real-time systems to embedded systems and distributed applications.

1.2 Setting Up Your Environment

Before we start writing Elixir code, we need to prepare your computer by setting up the necessary tools. Think of it as gathering your ingredients and utensils before starting a new recipe. Fortunately, setting up your Elixir development environment is a straightforward process, even for those new to programming.

1. Install Erlang:

Elixir runs on the Erlang Virtual Machine (BEAM).[1] Think of the BEAM as the foundation upon which Elixir code executes. It provides the runtime environment and manages resources for your Elixir applications.

To install Erlang, visit the official Erlang website (www.erlang.org) and download the installer for your operating system (Windows, macOS, or Linux). Follow the instructions provided to complete the installation.

2. Install Elixir:

Once you have Erlang installed, it's time to install Elixir itself. Head over to the official Elixir website (www.elixir-lang.org) and download the appropriate installer for your operating system. Again, follow the provided instructions to complete the installation.

3. Verify Installation:

After installing both Erlang and Elixir, it's a good idea to verify that everything is set up correctly. Open your terminal or command prompt and type the following command:

Bash

elixir -v

This command will display the installed Elixir version. If you see a version number, congratulations! You have successfully installed Elixir.

4. (Optional) Install an IDE or Text Editor:

While you can write Elixir code in any plain text editor, using an Integrated Development Environment (IDE) or a code editor with Elixir support can significantly improve your productivity. These tools offer features like syntax highlighting, code completion, debugging tools, and project management capabilities.[2]

Some popular choices for Elixir development include:

- **Visual Studio Code:** A free and versatile code editor with excellent Elixir support through extensions like ElixirLS.[3]
- **IntelliJ IDEA:** A powerful IDE with a plugin for Elixir development.

- **Atom:** Another free and customizable code editor with Elixir support.[4]
- **Emacs:** A highly extensible text editor with a dedicated Elixir mode.

Choose the editor that best suits your preferences and workflow.

5. Explore the Interactive Shell (IEx):

Elixir comes with a handy tool called IEx (Interactive Elixir).[5] It's an interactive shell where you can experiment with Elixir code, test functions, and see the results immediately.

To start IEx, simply open your terminal and type `iex`. You'll be greeted with a prompt where you can enter Elixir expressions.

For example, try typing `2 + 2` and press Enter. IEx will evaluate the expression and display the result: `4`.

IEx is a valuable tool for learning Elixir and exploring its features.[6] We'll be using it throughout this book to illustrate concepts and try out code snippets.

That's it! You've successfully set up your Elixir development environment. You're now ready to start writing and running Elixir code. In the next section, we'll take a closer look at the basic syntax and data types in Elixir.

1.3 Basic Syntax and Data Types

Now that your Elixir environment is set up, let's explore the building blocks of the language: its syntax and data types. Think of syntax as the grammar of Elixir, the rules that govern how you write code. Data types, on the other hand, are the different kinds of values that your code can manipulate, like numbers, text, and collections of data.

Basic Syntax

Elixir's syntax is designed to be clear, concise, and readable. It draws inspiration from Ruby, known for its elegant syntax, while incorporating elements of functional programming.

Here are a few key aspects of Elixir syntax:

- **Variables:** You store data in variables using the = sign. For example, name = "Alice" assigns the string "Alice" to the variable name.
- **Function Calls:** You call functions by writing the function name followed by parentheses, like IO.puts("Hello!"). This calls the puts function from the IO module to print "Hello!" to the console.
- **Operators:** Elixir uses familiar operators like +, -, *, / for arithmetic, and ==, !=, >, < for comparison.
- **Terminating Expressions:** In Elixir, you don't need semicolons (;) to end statements. Newlines generally indicate the end of an expression.

Data Types

Elixir provides a variety of built-in data types to represent different kinds of values:

- **Numbers:**
  - **Integers:** Whole numbers, like 10, –5, 1000.
  - **Floats:** Numbers with decimal points, like 3.14, –2.5.
- **Strings:** Sequences of characters enclosed in double quotes, like "Hello, Elixir!".
- **Atoms:** Constants that represent names. They start with a colon, like :ok, :error, :user. Atoms are often used to represent states or conditions.
- **Booleans:** Represent truth values, either true or false.
- **Lists:** Ordered collections of values, like [1, 2, 3] or ["apple", "banana", "cherry"]. Lists can contain elements of different data types.
- **Tuples:** Fixed-size collections of values, like {1, 2, 3}. Tuples are often used to group related data.
- **Maps:** Store key-value pairs, like %{name: "Alice", age: 30}. Maps are useful for representing structured data.

Example

Let's see these elements in action with a simple example:

Elixir

```
name = "Bob"  # Assign the string "Bob" to the variable name
age = 25    # Assign the integer 25 to the variable age
IO.puts("Hello, #{name}! You are #{age} years old.")
```

This code snippet demonstrates variable assignment, string concatenation using #{} (string interpolation), and calling the **IO.puts** function to print a formatted string to the console.

Understanding Immutability

A core concept in Elixir is immutability. This means that once you create a data structure (like a list or a map), you cannot modify it directly. Instead, any operation that seems like a modification actually creates a new data structure with the updated values.

For example, if you have a list **list = [1, 2, 3]** and you want to add an element, you would create a new list like this: **new_list = [0 | list]**. This results in **new_list** being [0, 1, 2, 3] while **list** remains [1, 2, 3].

Immutability might seem strange at first, but it offers significant advantages in terms of code predictability, concurrency safety, and easier debugging. We'll explore immutability further in later chapters.

1.4 Immutability and Its Implications

Immutability is a cornerstone of Elixir and functional programming in general. It means that once you create a data structure (like a list, tuple, or map), its value cannot be changed. This might seem counterintuitive if you're coming from languages where modifying data in place is the norm, but immutability brings significant advantages to Elixir programs.

Understanding Immutability

Let's illustrate with an example. In many languages, if you have a **list numbers** = [1, 2, 3] and you want to add the number 4 to the end, you might do something like numbers.append(4). This modifies the numbers list directly.

In Elixir, things work differently. If you have a list numbers = [1, 2, 3] and want to add 4, you would create a *new* list that includes the new value. For instance, new_numbers = numbers ++ [4] would create new_numbers as [1, 2, 3, 4] while leaving the original numbers list untouched.

Implications of Immutability

Immutability has profound implications for how you write and reason about Elixir code:

- **Predictability:** Since data structures cannot change unexpectedly, your code becomes more predictable. You can be confident that a variable holding a list will always hold that same list, not a mutated version. This makes it easier to understand the flow of data in your program and reduces the chance of unexpected side effects.
- **Concurrency Made Easier:** Immutability greatly simplifies concurrent programming. In concurrent systems, multiple processes often access and manipulate shared data. With mutable data, this can lead to race conditions and other concurrency bugs. Since Elixir data is immutable, these problems are largely avoided. Processes can operate on data without the risk of interfering with each other.

- **Simplified Debugging:** Debugging becomes easier when you know your data isn't changing unexpectedly. You can trace the flow of data through your program with confidence, making it simpler to identify the source of errors.
- **Efficient Data Sharing:** While it might seem like immutability would lead to a lot of data copying, the Erlang VM (BEAM) employs clever techniques to optimize this. It uses structural sharing, where new data structures share common parts with the old ones, minimizing memory usage and improving performance.

Examples of Immutability in Action

Let's see a few more examples of how immutability works in Elixir:

- **Updating a Map:** To update a value in a map, you create a new map with the updated key-value pair:

Elixir

```
map = %{name: "Alice", age: 30}
new_map = %{map | age: 31}  # new_map is %{name: "Alice", age: 31}
```

- **Adding to a List:** As seen earlier, you can add elements to a list by creating a new list:

Elixir

```
list = [1, 2, 3]
new_list = list ++ [4]  # new_list is [1, 2, 3, 4]
```

Embracing the Paradigm Shift

Immutability might require a shift in thinking if you're accustomed to mutable data structures. However, the benefits it brings in terms of code clarity, concurrency safety, and debugging efficiency make it a crucial aspect of Elixir. As you become more familiar with Elixir, you'll appreciate how immutability contributes to building robust and maintainable applications.

1.5 First Steps with IEx

Now that you have a basic understanding of Elixir's syntax and data types, it's time to get some hands-on experience with the language. Elixir provides an interactive shell called IEx (Interactive Elixir) that allows you to experiment with code, test functions, and explore the language in a REPL (Read-Eval-Print Loop) environment. Think of it as a playground for Elixir, where you can try things out and see the results immediately.

Starting IEx

To start IEx, open your terminal or command prompt and simply type iex. You'll be greeted with a prompt like this:

Erlang/OTP 25 [erts-13.1.2] [source] [64-bit] [smp:8:8] [ds:8:8:10] [async-threads:1] [jit]

Interactive Elixir (1.14.0) – press Ctrl+C to exit (type h()
ENTER for help)
iex(1)>

This indicates that IEx is ready for your input. The **iex(1)>** is
the prompt where you'll type your Elixir code.

Basic Interactions

Let's try some simple expressions:

Elixir

```
iex(1)> 2 + 2
4
iex(2)> "Hello" <> " " <> "Elixir!"
"Hello Elixir!"
iex(3)> String.length("Elixir")
6
```

As you can see, IEx evaluates the expressions you enter and
displays the results. You can perform arithmetic operations,
manipulate strings, and call functions, all within the IEx
environment.

Defining Variables

You can also define variables in IEx:

Elixir

```
iex(4)> name = "Alice"
"Alice"
iex(5)> age = 30
30
```

```
iex(6)> IO.puts("Hello, #{name}! You are #{age} years
old.")
Hello, Alice! You are 30 years old.
:ok
```

This code defines two variables, name and age, and then uses them in a string interpolation to print a greeting.

Helpful Commands

IEx provides a range of helpful commands to assist you in your exploration. Type h() to see a list of available commands. Here are a few useful ones:

- **h(Module)**: Displays documentation for a specific module. For example, **h(String)** shows documentation for the String module.
- **i(Term)**: Shows information about a data type or variable. For example, **i("hello")** provides information about the string "hello".
- **c(File)**: Compiles an Elixir file.
- **b()** : Displays a list of all bound variables.

Exploring Modules and Functions

IEx is a great way to explore Elixir's modules and functions. For instance, try typing **h(List)** to see the documentation for the List module, which provides functions for working with lists. You can then experiment with those functions directly in IEx.

Exiting IEx

To exit IEx, press Ctrl+C twice, or type **System.halt()** and press Enter.

IEx as a Learning Tool

IEx is an invaluable tool for learning and experimenting with Elixir. Use it to:

- Test code snippets and see how they work.
- Explore the functionality of different modules and functions.
- Experiment with different approaches to solving problems.
- Quickly verify the behavior of language constructs.

As you progress through this book, we'll frequently use IEx to illustrate concepts and try out code examples. Make IEx your friend, and it will serve you well on your Elixir journey.

Chapter 2: Functional Programming with Elixir

Welcome to the exciting world of functional programming with Elixir! In this chapter, we'll explore some of the core concepts that make Elixir such a powerful and expressive language. We'll learn about pattern matching, a fundamental technique for working with data in Elixir; functions and modules, the building blocks of Elixir programs; and higher-order functions, which allow us to write more concise and reusable code. We'll also touch upon recursion, the Elixir way to perform loops, and guards and conditionals, which enable us to control the flow of execution in our programs.

2.1 Pattern Matching: The Cornerstone of Elixir

Alright, let's talk about one of Elixir's most powerful and fundamental features: pattern matching! Think of it as a supercharged way of comparing data and extracting values. It's like having a set of stencils that you can use to check if your data fits a certain shape, and if it does, you can grab specific parts of it.

The Match Operator (=)

In Elixir, the equals sign (=) isn't just for assigning values. It's actually a **match operator**. When you write something like x = 5, you're not just saying "put the value 5 into the variable x." You're saying "check if the pattern x matches the value 5." Since x is a variable, it's a wildcard that matches anything, so the match succeeds, and 5 gets bound to x.

Matching Simple Values

This matching behavior gets more interesting when we work with different data types. Let's try it in IEx:

Elixir

```
iex(1)> 5 = 5
5
iex(2)> 5 = 6
** (MatchError) no match of right hand side value: 6
```

In the first case, the match succeeds because both sides are the same value. But in the second case, we get a MatchError because 5 does not match 6.

Matching Complex Data

The real power of pattern matching shines when you work with more complex data structures like lists, tuples, and maps.

1. Matching Lists:

Imagine you have a list of numbers, and you want to grab the first number and the rest of the list separately. Pattern matching makes this super easy:

Elixir

```
iex(1)> [head | tail] = [1, 2, 3, 4]
[1, 2, 3, 4]
iex(2)> head
1
iex(3)> tail
[2, 3, 4]
```

Here, [head | tail] is a pattern that matches any list with at least one element. The **head** variable captures the **first** element, and **tail** captures the remaining list.

2. Matching Tuples:

Let's say you have a tuple representing a person's name and age:

Elixir

```
iex(1)> {name, age} = {"Bob", 30}
{"Bob", 30}
iex(2)> name
"Bob"
iex(3)> age
30
```

The pattern {name, age} matches any tuple with two elements, binding the first element to **name** and the second to **age**.

3. Matching Maps:

You can also use pattern matching to extract values from maps:

Elixir

```
iex(1)> %{name: person_name, age: person_age} =
%{name: "Alice", age: 25}
%{age: 25, name: "Alice"}
iex(2)> person_name
"Alice"
iex(3)> person_age
25
```

In this case, we're matching a map with specific keys (**name** and **age**) and capturing their corresponding values in the **person_name** and **person_age** variables.

Pattern Matching in Function Clauses

One of the most common uses of pattern matching is in function definitions. You can define multiple function clauses with different patterns, and Elixir will execute the clause that matches the given arguments.

Elixir

```
defmodule Greeter do
def greet("Alice") do
IO.puts("Hello, Alice! You're special.")
end
def greet(name) do
IO.puts("Hello, #{name}!")
end
end
```

In this example, if you call **Greeter.greet("Alice")**, the first clause will match and execute. For any other name, the second clause will be used.

Pin Operator (∧)

Sometimes you want to match against the existing value of a variable, rather than rebinding it. This is where the pin operator (∧) comes in handy.

Elixir

```
iex(1)> x = 1
1
iex(2)> x = 2
2
iex(3)> ^x = 2
2
iex(4)> ^x = 3
** (MatchError) no match of right hand side value: 3
```

In this example, ∧x = 2 matches because x is already bound to 2. But ∧x = 3 fails because it's trying to match the *value* of x (which is 2) against 3.

Why Pattern Matching Matters

Pattern matching is a core part of Elixir's elegance and power. It allows you to write concise, expressive code that's easy to read and reason about. As you continue your Elixir journey, you'll find pattern matching used extensively in various contexts, from function definitions and conditional logic to error handling and data manipulation. So embrace it, play with it in IEx, and watch your Elixir code become more elegant and powerful!

2.2 Functions and Modules

Let's talk about how to structure your Elixir code effectively using functions and modules! Think of functions as the verbs of your program – they're the actions that make things happen. Modules, on the other hand, are like containers that help you organize your functions and keep your code neat and tidy.

Defining Functions

In Elixir, you define a function using the def keyword, followed by the function name, arguments in parentheses, and the function body enclosed in do...end blocks.

Elixir

```
defmodule MyModule do
def greet(name) do
IO.puts("Hello, #{name}!")
end
end
```

This code defines a module named **MyModule** (we'll talk more about modules shortly) and a function called **greet** that takes one argument (name) and prints a friendly greeting to the console.

To call this function, you'd use **MyModule.greet("Alice")**, which would print "Hello, Alice!".

Function Clauses and Pattern Matching

One of the cool things about Elixir functions is that you can define multiple "clauses" for the same function, each with different patterns. Elixir will intelligently choose the clause that matches the arguments you provide.

Elixir

```elixir
defmodule MyModule do
def greet(:english, name) do
IO.puts("Hello, #{name}!")
end
def greet(:spanish, name) do
IO.puts("Hola, #{name}!")
end
end
```

Now, **MyModule.greet(:english, "Bob")** prints "Hello, Bob!", while **MyModule.greet(:spanish, "Bob")** prints "Hola, Bob!". This allows you to create flexible and expressive functions.

Function Naming Conventions

In Elixir, function names (and variable names) should be in snake_case (all lowercase with underscores separating words). This keeps your code consistent and easy to read.

Modules: Your Code Organizers

As your Elixir projects grow, you'll want a way to organize your code and prevent naming collisions (having two functions with the same name). That's where modules come in!

Think of modules as containers for your functions. They provide namespaces, so you can have functions with the same name in different modules without any conflicts.

Elixir

```elixir
defmodule Math do
def add(x, y) do
x + y
end
def subtract(x, y) do
x - y
end
end
defmodule StringHelper do
def reverse(string) do
String.reverse(string)
end
end
```

Now you can call Math.add(2, 3) and StringHelper.reverse("hello") without any ambiguity.

Why Use Modules?

- **Organization:** Modules help you group related functions, making your code easier to navigate and understand.

- **Namespaces:** They prevent naming conflicts, allowing you to use common function names like start, stop, or process in different contexts.
- **Code Reusability:** You can easily reuse modules across different projects.

Calling Functions from Other Modules

To use a function from another module, you simply use the module name followed by the function name, like Module.function_name(arguments).

Exploring Built-in Modules

Elixir comes with a rich set of built-in modules that provide a wide range of functionality. Some commonly used modules include:

- IO: For input/output operations like printing to the console.
- String: For working with strings.
- List: For manipulating lists.
- Map: For working with maps.
- Enum: For working with enumerables (lists, maps, etc.).

You can explore these modules and their functions using IEx. For example, try h(String) in IEx to see the documentation for the String module.

By effectively using functions and modules, you can create well-structured, maintainable, and reusable Elixir code. As you progress through this book, you'll see how these concepts are applied in building real-world applications.

2.3 Higher-Order Functions

Let's talk about higher-order functions! These are functions that can take other functions as arguments or return functions as results. They[1] might sound a bit abstract at first, but they're incredibly powerful tools for writing concise and reusable code. Think of them as functions that operate on other functions, kind of like how a conductor guides an orchestra.

Why Higher-Order Functions?

Higher-order functions allow you to abstract away common patterns of data manipulation. Instead of writing the same loops and conditional logic over and over again, you can use higher-order functions to express your intent more clearly and concisely.

Key Higher-Order Functions in Elixir

Elixir provides a bunch of useful higher-order functions, especially in the Enum and Stream modules. Let's explore three of the most common ones: map, reduce, and filter.

1. Enum.map

Imagine you have a list of numbers, and you want to square each number. You could write a loop to iterate over the list and calculate the square of each element. But with Enum.map, it's much simpler:

Elixir

```
iex> list = [1, 2, 3, 4]
[1, 2, 3, 4]
iex> Enum.map(list, fn x -> x * x end)
[1, 4, 9, 16]
```

Enum.map takes two arguments: the list you want to transform and a function that defines the transformation. In this case, the anonymous function fn x -> x * x end takes a number x and returns its square. Enum.map applies this function to each element in the list and returns a new list with the transformed values.

2. Enum.reduce

Let's say you want to calculate the sum of all numbers in a list. Again, you could use a loop, but Enum.reduce provides a more elegant solution:

Elixir

```
iex> list = [1, 2, 3, 4]
[1, 2, 3, 4]
iex> Enum.reduce(list, 0, fn x, acc -> x + acc end)
10
```

Enum.reduce takes three arguments:

- The list you want to process.
- An initial accumulator value (in this case, 0).
- A function that takes an element from the list and the current accumulator value and returns the updated accumulator value.

The function **fn x, acc -> x + acc end** adds each element **x** to the accumulator **acc**. **Enum.reduce** iterates through the list, applying this function to each element and the accumulator, and finally returns the accumulated value (the sum in this case).

3. Enum.filter

Suppose you want to filter a list to keep only the even numbers. **Enum.filter** makes this a breeze:

Elixir

```
iex> list = [1, 2, 3, 4, 5]
[1, 2, 3, 4, 5]
iex> Enum.filter(list, fn x -> rem(x, 2) == 0 end)
[2, 4]
```

Enum.filter takes two arguments:

- The list you want to filter.
- A function that takes an element and returns **true** if the element should be kept, and **false** otherwise.

The function **fn x -> rem(x, 2) == 0 end** checks if a number x is even. **Enum.filter** applies this function to each element and returns a new list containing only the even numbers.

Benefits of Higher-Order Functions

- **Conciseness:** They allow you to express complex operations in a more compact and readable way.
- **Reusability:** You can reuse the same higher-order function with different functions to perform various transformations.

- **Abstraction:** They abstract away common patterns, making your code more focused on the intent rather than the implementation details.

As you become more comfortable with Elixir, you'll find that higher-order functions are essential tools for writing elegant and efficient code. So, embrace them, experiment with them, and watch your Elixir code become more powerful and expressive!

2.4 Recursion: The Elixir Way to Loop

Alright, let's talk about loops! But with a twist. In Elixir, you won't find familiar loop constructs like for or while. Instead, Elixir embraces the power of **recursion**. Think of recursion as a function calling itself, like a set of Russian nesting dolls, each one containing a smaller version of itself.

Why Recursion?

You might wonder, "Why recursion? Isn't it confusing?" Well, it might seem a bit unusual at first, but recursion is a natural fit for Elixir's functional style and immutability. Since you can't modify variables in place, recursion provides an elegant way to iterate over data and perform repetitive tasks.

How Recursion Works

Let's break down a simple example. Suppose you want to calculate the sum of all numbers in a list. Here's how you might do it with recursion:

Elixir

```elixir
defmodule MyModule do
def sum_list([], acc) do
 acc
end
def sum_list([head | tail], acc) do
sum_list(tail, acc + head)
end
end
```

Let's analyze this code step-by-step:

1. **Base Case:** The first function clause sum_list([], acc) is the **base case**. It matches an empty list ([]) and simply returns the accumulator (acc). This is crucial to stop the recursion.
2. **Recursive Case:** The second clause sum_list([head | tail], acc) matches a non-empty list. It uses pattern matching to extract the first element (head) and the rest of the list (tail). It then calls itself (sum_list) with the tail and an updated accumulator (acc + head).
3. **How it Works:** When you call MyModule.sum_list([1, 2, 3], 0), the second clause matches. It adds 1 (the head) to 0 (the acc) and calls sum_list([2, 3], 1). This process repeats, adding each element to the accumulator until it reaches the empty list. At that point, the base case kicks in and returns the final accumulated value (which is 6 in this case).

Tail Recursion

Elixir is smart about recursion. It optimizes **tail-recursive** functions, where the recursive call is the last operation in the function. This means that the recursive calls don't pile up on the call stack, preventing stack overflow errors even for deep recursion.

Benefits of Recursion in Elixir

- **Elegance:** Recursion often leads to more concise and readable code, especially when dealing with recursive data structures like lists and trees.
- **Immutability:** It aligns perfectly with Elixir's immutability, as you're creating new values with each recursive call instead of modifying existing ones.
- **Efficiency:** Elixir's tail-call optimization ensures that recursive functions are efficient and don't consume excessive memory.

When to Use Recursion

Recursion is particularly well-suited for tasks like:

- **Traversing data structures:** Walking through lists, trees, or graphs.
- **Mathematical calculations:** Implementing algorithms like factorial or Fibonacci sequences.
- **Processing data sequentially:** Applying a function to each element in a collection.

As you become more familiar with Elixir, you'll find that recursion is a natural and powerful way to express iterative logic. So, embrace the recursive approach, and watch your Elixir code become more elegant and efficient!

2.5 Guards and Conditionals

Let's talk about how to add some logic and control flow to your Elixir code! We'll explore guards and conditionals, which allow you to make your functions smarter and more flexible. Think of guards as bouncers at a club, checking if the arguments meet certain criteria before allowing them in. Conditionals, on the other hand, are like forks in the road, directing your code down different paths depending on certain conditions.

Guards:

Guards are expressions that you can add to function clauses to further refine pattern matching. They act as filters, ensuring that a clause only matches if the guard condition evaluates to true.

Elixir

```
defmodule MyModule do
def greet(name) when is_binary(name) do
IO.puts("Hello, #{name}!")
end
def greet(_) do
IO.puts("Hey there! I don't know your name, but greetings anyway!")
end
end
```

In this example, the first greet function clause has a guard when is_binary(name). This means it will only match if the name argument is a binary (which is how Elixir represents strings). If you call MyModule.greet("Alice"), the first clause matches. But if you call **MyModule.greet(123)**, the guard fails, and the second clause (with the wildcard _) matches instead.

Allowed Guard Expressions

You can use a variety of expressions in guards, but they have some limitations. Guards should be simple and fast to evaluate. They typically involve:

- **Type checks:** is_binary(name), is_integer(age), is_list(items)
- **Comparisons:** age >= 18, length(list) > 0
- **Arithmetic operations:** x + y < 10
- **Calls to certain built-in functions:** is_even(number)

Conditionals: Choosing Your Path

Elixir provides familiar conditional constructs like **if, else**, and cond to control the flow of execution based on conditions.

1. if **and** else

The if expression allows you to execute different code blocks based on a condition.

Elixir

iex> if true, do: "This will be printed", else: "This won't"
"This will be printed"

In this example, the condition true is always true, so the code in the do: block is executed. If the condition were false, the code in the else: block would be executed.

2. cond

The cond expression is like a series of if statements. It evaluates conditions sequentially and executes the code block associated with the first true condition.

Elixir

```
iex> cond do
...>  2 + 2 == 5 -> "This is false"
...>  2 * 2 == 4 -> "This is true"
...>  true -> "This is the default"
...> end
"This is true"
```

In this example, the first condition is false, so it moves to the second. The second condition is true, so the corresponding code block is executed. The true -> clause acts as a catch-all, ensuring that something is always executed.

Case Expressions

Elixir also has case expressions, which are similar to cond but use pattern matching for conditions.

Elixir

```
iex> case {1, 2} do
...>  {1, x} -> "Matched with x = #{x}"
...>  {x, 2} -> "Matched with x = #{x}"
...>  _ -> "No match"
...> end
"Matched with x = 2"
```

Why Guards and Conditionals Matter

Guards and conditionals are essential tools for writing flexible and expressive Elixir code. They allow you to:

- **Create functions that handle different input types and values.**
- **Implement complex logic and decision-making.**
- **Control the flow of execution in your programs.**

As you build more sophisticated Elixir applications, you'll find yourself using guards and conditionals extensively to create robust and maintainable code. So, experiment with these constructs, and see how they can empower your Elixir programming!

Chapter 3: Working with Data in Elixir

Now that we've covered some functional programming fundamentals, let's dive into how Elixir handles data! In this chapter, we'll explore the core data structures you'll use day-to-day: lists, tuples, and maps. We'll also look at how to define your own custom data types with structs, and how to work with text and binary data. Finally, we'll get a sneak peek at processes and message passing, a key concept in Elixir's concurrency model.

3.1 Lists, Tuples, and Maps

Let's explore how Elixir helps you organize and work with collections of data! Think of these data structures as different types of containers, each with its own unique features and purposes. We'll look at lists, tuples, and maps – the bread and butter of data handling in Elixir.

1. Lists: Your Ordered Collection

Imagine a to-do list, where each item has a specific position. That's essentially what a list is in Elixir – an ordered collection of values.

- **Creating Lists:** You create lists using square brackets []:

Elixir

```
iex> my_list = [1, 2, 3, "hello", :atom]
[1, 2, 3, "hello", :atom]
```

- **Key Features:**
    - **Ordered:** The elements have a defined sequence.
    - **Dynamic:** You can add or remove elements as needed.
    - **Versatile:** Lists can hold a mix of data types, like numbers, strings, atoms, even other lists!
- **Common Operations:**
    - **++ (Concatenation):** Combines two lists.

Elixir

```
iex> [1, 2] ++ [3, 4]
[1, 2, 3, 4]
```

- **-- (Difference):** Removes elements from a list.

Elixir

```
iex> [1, 2, 3, 4] -- [2, 4]
[1, 3]
```

- **[head | tail] (Head/Tail):** This is a powerful pattern matching technique to extract the first element (head) and the rest of the list (tail).

Elixir

```
iex> [head | tail] = [1, 2, 3]
[1, 2, 3]
iex> head
1
iex> tail
[2, 3]
```

2. Tuples: Fixed-Size Data Bundles

Think of tuples as containers with a fixed number of compartments. Each compartment holds a value, and the number of compartments is determined when you create the tuple.

- **Creating Tuples:** Use curly braces {}:

Elixir

```
iex> my_tuple = {123, "Main Street", :ok}
{123, "Main Street", :ok}
```

- **Key Features:**
    - **Fixed Size:** Once created, you can't add or remove elements.
    - **Efficient Access:** You can quickly access elements by their index (position).
    - **Grouping Related Data:** Tuples are often used to bundle related pieces of information, like coordinates, database records, or function return values.
- **Common Operations:**
    - **elem(tuple, index):** Retrieves an element at a specific index.

Elixir

```
iex> my_tuple = {:ok, "Success", 200}
{:ok, "Success", 200}
iex> elem(my_tuple, 1)
"Success"
```

> ○ **put_elem(tuple, index, value)**: Creates a new tuple with an updated value at a specific index. Remember, tuples are immutable, so this creates a new tuple, not modify the original.

Elixir

```
iex> put_elem(my_tuple, 2, 201)
{:ok, "Success", 201}
```

3. Maps: Key-Value Storage

Maps are like dictionaries – they store data in key-value pairs. You can quickly look up a value by its associated key.

- **Creating Maps:** Use %{}:

Elixir

```
iex> my_map = %{name: "Alice", age: 30, city: "New York"}
%{age: 30, city: "New York", name: "Alice"}
```

- **Key Features:**

- ○ **Key-Value Based:** Each value is associated with a unique key.
  - ○ **Efficient Lookup:** You can quickly find a value using its key.
  - ○ **Dynamic:** You can add or remove key-value pairs.
- **Common Operations:**
  - ○ **map.key** or **map[:key]:** Accesses the value associated with a key.

Elixir

```
iex> my_map.age
30
iex> my_map[:city]
"New York"
```

- ○ %{map | key: new_value}: Creates a new map with an updated value for a specific key.

Elixir

```
iex> %{my_map | age: 31}
%{age: 31, city: "New York", name: "Alice"}
```

Choosing the Right Data Structure

- **Lists:** When you need an ordered collection and the number of elements might change.

- **Tuples:** When you have a fixed number of elements with specific meanings, and you need efficient access by index.
- **Maps:** When you need to store data as key-value pairs and perform lookups by key.

As you gain more experience with Elixir, you'll develop an intuition for which data structure is best suited for different situations. So, experiment with lists, tuples, and maps, and see how they can help you organize and manipulate your data effectively!

3.2 Structs:

Let's level up your data handling skills by learning about structs! Think of structs as blueprints for creating your own custom data types. They allow you to group related data together and give it a meaningful name. It's like creating a new kind of container specifically designed to hold the information you need.

Why Use Structs?

- **Organization:** Structs help you organize related data into a single unit, making your code cleaner and easier to understand.
- **Clarity:** By giving your data types meaningful names, you improve the readability of your code and make it more self-documenting.

- **Compile-Time Checks:** Structs provide compile-time checks, meaning the compiler will catch errors if you try to access fields that don't exist or assign incorrect data types.
- **Default Values:** You can provide default values for struct fields, ensuring that your data is always in a valid state.

Defining Structs

You define a struct using the **defstruct** keyword within a module. Let's create a struct to represent a user:

Elixir

```
defmodule User do
defstruct name: "", age: 0, email: ""
end
```

This code defines a struct named User with three fields: **name**, **age**, and **email**. Each field has a default value: an empty string for name and **email**, and 0 for age.

Creating Structs

To create an instance of a struct, you use the % symbol followed by the struct name and a set of key-value pairs for the fields:

Elixir

```
iex> %User{}
%User{age: 0, email: "", name: ""}
iex> %User{name: "Bob", age: 25}
%User{age: 25, email: "", name: "Bob"}
```

The first example creates a **User** struct with all default values. The second example creates a **User** struct with specific values for **name** and **age**, while **email** uses the default value.

Accessing Fields

You can access the fields of a struct using dot notation:

Elixir

```
iex> user = %User{name: "Alice", age: 30}
%User{age: 30, email: "", name: "Alice"}
iex> user.name
"Alice"
iex> user.age
30
```

Updating Fields

To update a field in a struct, you create a new struct with the updated value. Remember, structs are immutable, so you're not modifying the original struct.

Elixir

```
iex> updated_user = %{user | age: 31}
%User{age: 31, email: "", name: "Alice"}
iex> user.age
30
iex> updated_user.age
31
```

Pattern Matching with Structs

You can use pattern matching to extract values from structs or match against specific struct values:

Elixir

```
iex> %User{name: user_name} = %User{name: "Bob", age: 25}
%User{age: 25, email: "", name: "Bob"}
iex> user_name
"Bob"
```

Benefits of Structs

- **Data Integrity:** Structs help ensure that your data is consistent and valid by providing default values and compile-time checks.
- **Code Readability:** They make your code more readable and self-documenting by giving meaningful names to your data types.
- **Maintainability:** Structs make it easier to maintain and update your code because they provide a clear structure for your data.

As you work on more complex Elixir projects, you'll find that structs are invaluable for modeling and managing your data effectively. So, embrace the power of structs, and watch your Elixir code become more organized, robust, and maintainable!

3.3 Working with Strings and Binaries

Let's talk about how Elixir handles text and binary data! In Elixir, text is represented as strings, while raw bytes of data are represented as binaries. Both are essential for various tasks, from handling user input and displaying information to working with files and network communication.

Strings: Representing Text

Strings in Elixir are sequences of characters enclosed in double quotes. They're your go-to for working with text.

- **Creating Strings:**

Elixir

```
iex> my_string = "Hello, Elixir!"
"Hello, Elixir!"
```

- **String Interpolation:** You can embed variables or expressions within strings using #{}:

Elixir

```
iex> name = "Alice"
"Alice"
iex> "Hello, #{name}! It's #{Time.new()}."
"Hello, Alice! It's ~U[2024-12-01 12:29:34.776890Z]."
```

This allows you to dynamically construct strings with variable values.

- **Common String Operations:**

Elixir provides a powerful **String** module with a wide range of functions for manipulating strings. Here are a few examples:

* **`String.length(string)`:** Returns the length of a string.

```elixir
iex> String.length("Elixir")
6
```

* **`String.upcase(string)`** and `String.downcase(string)`:** Converts a string to uppercase or lowercase.

```elixir
iex> String.upcase("elixir")
"ELIXIR"
```

* **`String.split(string, pattern)`:** Splits a string into a list of substrings based on a pattern.

```elixir
iex> String.split("hello world", " ")
["hello", "world"]
```

* **`String.trim(string)`:** Removes leading and trailing whitespace from a string.

```elixir
iex> String.trim(" hello ")
"hello"
```

You can explore more string functions in IEx by typing h(String).

Binaries: Handling Raw Bytes

Binaries are sequences of bytes. They're used to represent raw data, such as images, audio files, or network packets.

- **Creating Binaries:** You create binaries using << >>:

Elixir

```
iex> my_binary = <<1, 2, 3, 4>>
<<1, 2, 3, 4>>
iex> <<head, rest::binary>> = <<1, 2, 3, 4>>
<<1, 2, 3, 4>>
iex> head
1
iex> rest
<<2, 3, 4>>
```

- **Key Concepts:**
  - **Bytes:** Binaries are composed of bytes, where each byte is an 8-bit value (ranging from 0 to 255).
  - **Bitstrings:** Binaries are a type of bitstring, which is a more general way to represent sequences of bits.
- **Common Operations:**

- **Pattern Matching:** You can use pattern matching to extract data from binaries, as shown in the example above.
- **Binary Concatenation:** You can concatenate binaries using <>:

```
iex> <<1, 2>> <> <<3, 4>>
<<1, 2, 3, 4>>
```

- **Bitwise Operations:** Elixir provides bitwise operators like &&& (and), ||| (or), and ∧∧∧ (xor) for manipulating binary data at the bit level.

Strings vs. Binaries

While strings are technically binaries in Elixir, they have a specific encoding (UTF-8) that ensures they represent valid text. Binaries, on the other hand, can hold any sequence of bytes, regardless of whether they represent valid text.

When to Use Strings and Binaries

- **Strings:** When you're working with text, such as user input, filenames, or messages.
- **Binaries:** When you're dealing with raw data, such as images, audio files, network packets, or encoded data.

By understanding how to work with strings and binaries, you'll be well-equipped to handle a wide range of data manipulation tasks in Elixir. So, experiment with these data types and explore the powerful functions provided by the String module and the bitwise operators to become proficient in handling text and binary data in your Elixir applications.

3.4 Processes and Message Passing: A First Look

Let's get a glimpse into one of the most exciting aspects of Elixir: its concurrency model! Elixir leverages the Erlang Virtual Machine (BEAM), which is famous for its ability to handle massive concurrency with ease. This is achieved through processes and message passing.

What are Processes?

Think of processes as lightweight, independent workers within your Elixir application. They're like tiny, self-contained programs running concurrently, each with its own memory and state. Unlike threads in many other languages, processes in Elixir are isolated from each other, making them incredibly robust and fault-tolerant.

Message Passing:

Processes communicate with each other by sending and receiving messages. It's like sending letters or emails − each process has a "mailbox" where it can receive messages from other processes. This message-passing mechanism is the key to building concurrent and distributed systems in Elixir.

Spawning Processes

You can create (or "spawn") a new process using the spawn function. Let's try it in IEx:

Elixir

```
iex> pid = spawn(fn -> IO.puts("Hello from a process!") end)
#PID<0.100.0>
Hello from a process!
```

This code does the following:

1. **spawn(fn -> ... end):** The spawn function takes an anonymous function as an argument. This function defines the code that the new process will execute.
2. **IO.puts("Hello from a process!"):** This is the code that will run in the new process. It simply prints a message to the console.
3. **pid = ...:** The spawn function returns a process identifier (PID), which is a unique reference to the newly created process. We store this PID in the variable pid.

Sending Messages

You can send messages to a process using its PID and the send function:

Elixir

```
iex> send(pid, :hello)
:hello
```

This code sends the atom :hello as a message to the process identified by pid.

Receiving Messages

To receive messages within a process, you use the receive block. Here's a simple example:

Elixir

```
defmodule MyProcess do
def start do
receive do
:hello -> IO.puts("Received :hello")
:world -> IO.puts("Received :world")
end
end
end

iex> pid = spawn(MyProcess, :start, [])
#PID<0.92.0>
iex> send(pid, :hello)
:hello
Received :hello
iex> send(pid, :world)
:world
Received :world
```

In this example:

1. We define a module **MyProcess** with a **start** function.
2. The **start** function uses a **receive** block to wait for messages.

3. Inside the **receive** block, we use pattern matching to handle different messages. If the process receives the atom :hello, it prints "Received :hello". If it receives :world, it prints "Received :world".

4. We spawn a new process that executes **MyProcess.start**.

5. We send messages :hello and :world to the process, and it responds accordingly.

Why Processes and Message Passing Matter

Processes and message passing are fundamental to Elixir's concurrency model. They allow you to:

- **Build highly concurrent systems:** Handle many tasks simultaneously without the risks associated with shared memory and mutable state.
- **Create fault-tolerant applications:** Isolate failures to prevent cascading errors and build resilient systems.
- **Develop distributed systems:** Distribute your application across multiple nodes for scalability and reliability.

This was just a taste of processes and message passing. We'll delve deeper into these concepts in later chapters, exploring how to use them to build robust and concurrent Elixir applications. For now, keep in mind that processes and message passing are essential tools in your Elixir toolbox, enabling you to create applications that are fast, reliable, and scalable.

Chapter 4: Building Blocks of Elixir Applications

It's time to start building some serious Elixir applications! In this chapter, we'll explore OTP (Open Telecom Platform), a powerful set of tools and libraries that form the foundation of robust, fault-tolerant Elixir systems. We'll learn about processes, supervisors, and applications, the core components of OTP. Then, we'll dive into GenServer, a powerful behavior for building stateful processes. Finally, we'll put it all together to create a basic OTP application and learn how to test it with ExUnit.

4.1 Introduction to OTP:

Okay, time to unlock the power of OTP (Open Telecom Platform)! OTP might sound a bit mysterious, but it's really just a set of tools and principles that help you build rock-solid, fault-tolerant Elixir applications. Think of OTP as your trusty sidekick, providing structure and guidance for managing processes, handling errors, and organizing your code.

Processes:

We've already met processes in the previous chapter. Remember those lightweight, independent workers that run concurrently within your application? They're like little self-contained programs, each with its own memory and state. The beauty of processes is that they're isolated from each other. If one process crashes, it won't bring down the whole system – kind of like how a single bulb burning out doesn't cause the entire house to lose power.

Supervisors:

Now, imagine you have a bunch of these processes running, each doing its own thing. How do you make sure they're all behaving and doing their jobs? That's where supervisors come in! Supervisors are special processes that monitor other processes (their "children"). If a child process misbehaves and crashes, the supervisor can automatically restart it, ensuring your application stays up and running smoothly. It's like having a babysitter that keeps an eye on the kids and makes sure they don't get into too much trouble.

Applications:

Applications are the top-level containers for your Elixir code. They group together modules and processes, providing a structure for organizing and managing your application's components. Think of an application as a house that holds all the rooms (modules) and people (processes) living in it.

OTP in Action: A Simple Analogy

Let's imagine you're running a restaurant.

- **Processes:** Your chefs, waiters, and cashiers are like processes. They each have specific tasks and work concurrently to keep the restaurant running.
- **Supervisors:** The manager is like a supervisor. They oversee the staff, making sure everyone is doing their

job and handling any issues that arise. If a chef gets sick, the manager finds a replacement to keep the kitchen running.

- **Application:** The restaurant itself is the application. It provides the structure and environment for all the staff and processes to work together.

Benefits of OTP

By combining processes, supervisors, and applications, OTP provides a structured approach to building applications that are:

- **Concurrent:** Handle many customers (requests) simultaneously.
- **Fault-tolerant:** Recover from errors gracefully (like a chef burning a dish).
- **Scalable:** Handle increasing traffic as your restaurant becomes popular.
- **Maintainable:** Easy to manage and update as your menu and staff change.

OTP in Code (A Sneak Peek)

While we'll dive deeper into OTP in the following sections, here's a quick taste of how it looks in code:

Elixir

```elixir
# In your application's supervisor module
def start(_type, _args) do
children = [
# Define the processes to be supervised
]
Supervisor.start_link(children, strategy: :one_for_one)
```

end

This code snippet shows how you define a supervisor that starts and monitors child processes.

OTP is a powerful toolset for building robust and scalable Elixir applications. By understanding its core concepts, you'll be well-equipped to create systems that can handle real-world challenges and provide a great user experience. So, embrace OTP, and watch your Elixir applications become more reliable and maintainable!

4.2 GenServer

One of the most important building blocks in OTP! GenServer stands for "Generic Server," and it's a powerful tool for building stateful processes. Think of GenServer as a template or blueprint that provides a standard way to create processes that can:

- **Maintain state:** Store and manage data over time.
- **Handle messages:** Receive and respond to messages from other processes.
- **Perform actions:** Execute code in response to messages or internal events.

Why GenServer?

GenServer simplifies the process of building stateful processes by providing a structured approach and handling a lot of the low-level details for you. It's like having a helpful assistant that takes care of the tedious tasks, allowing you to focus on the core logic of your process.

Key GenServer Concepts

Let's break down the key concepts of GenServer:

- **State:** This is the data that your GenServer holds and manages. It can be any Elixir data structure, like a number, a list, a map, or even a custom struct.
- **Callbacks:** These are functions that you define within your GenServer module to handle different types of messages and events. GenServer provides a set of predefined callbacks, such as init, handle_call, handle_cast, and terminate, that you can implement to customize your GenServer's behavior.
- start_link: This is a function that you use to start your GenServer and link it to the current process. Linking ensures that if the current process crashes, the GenServer will also be terminated, preventing orphaned processes.
- call **and** cast: These are functions used to send messages to a GenServer. call sends a synchronous message, meaning the sender waits for a reply. cast sends an asynchronous message, meaning the sender doesn't wait for a reply (fire and forget).

Building a GenServer: Step-by-Step

Let's build a simple GenServer that manages a counter. This GenServer will allow us to increment the counter and retrieve its current value.

1. **Define the Module:**

Elixir

```elixir
defmodule Counter do
use GenServer
# ... (Callbacks and functions will go here) ...
end
```

We define a module named **Counter** and use the **use GenServer** macro to include the GenServer functionality.

2. **Implement the start_link Function:**

Elixir

```elixir
def start_link(initial_value) do
GenServer.start_link(__MODULE__,        initial_value,
name: __MODULE__)
end
```

This function starts the GenServer with an initial value and gives it a name (in this case, the module name itself).

3. **Define the init Callback:**

Elixir

```elixir
def init(value) do
{:ok, value}
end
```

The **init** callback is called when the GenServer starts. It receives the initial value and returns **{:ok, value}** to indicate successful initialization.

4. **Implement** handle_call **and** handle_cast **Callbacks:**

Elixir

```elixir
def handle_call(:value, _from, state) do
{:reply, state, state}
end
def handle_cast(:increment, state) do
{:noreply, state + 1}
end
```

- o **handle_call** handles synchronous messages. In this case, it responds to the message :value by returning the current state (the counter value).
- o **handle_cast** handles asynchronous messages. It responds to the message :increment by incrementing the counter value in the state.

5. **Add Helper Functions:**

Elixir

```elixir
def increment do
GenServer.cast(__MODULE__, :increment)
end
def value do
GenServer.call(__MODULE__, :value)
end
```

These functions provide a convenient way to interact with the GenServer from outside the module. increment casts an :increment message, and value calls the GenServer to get the current value.

Using the GenServer

Now, let's try out our **Counter** GenServer in IEx:

Elixir

```
iex> Counter.start_link(0)
{:ok, #PID<0.100.0>}
iex> Counter.value()
0
iex> Counter.increment()
:ok
iex> Counter.value()
1
iex> Counter.increment()
:ok
iex> Counter.value()
2
```

As you can see, we can start the GenServer, increment the counter, and retrieve its value.

GenServer provides a powerful and structured way to build stateful processes in Elixir. By understanding its core concepts and callbacks, you can create concurrent and fault-tolerant applications that manage state effectively. So, embrace GenServer, experiment with it, and watch your Elixir applications become more robust and dynamic!

4.3 Building a Basic OTP Application

Alright, let's put together what we've learned about OTP and GenServer to build a basic OTP application! This will give you a hands-on understanding of how to structure a simple Elixir application using processes, supervisors, and applications.

Setting the Stage: Our Application's Purpose

Our application will be very simple. It will:

1. **Start a supervisor:** This supervisor will be responsible for monitoring our processes.
2. **Start a Counter GenServer:** This GenServer will be the worker process in our application, managing a counter value (the same one we created in the previous section).

Step 1: Create the Application Module

First, let's create a module for our application. By convention, this module is usually named **MyApp.Application** (replace **MyApp** with your application's name).

Elixir

```elixir
defmodule MyApp.Application do
use Application
def start(_type, _args) do
# ... (Supervisor and child processes will be defined here) ...
end
```

end

We use the **use Application** macro to include the necessary functionality for defining an OTP application. The **start** function is the entry point for our application. It will be called when the application starts.

Step 2: Define the Supervisor

Inside the start function, we'll define our supervisor and the child processes it will supervise.

Elixir

```elixir
def start(_type, _args) do
children = [
{Counter, 0}
]
opts = [strategy: :one_for_one, name: MyApp.Supervisor]
Supervisor.start_link(children, opts)
end
```

Let's break this down:

- **children** = [...]: This list defines the child processes that the supervisor will manage. In our case, we have a single child: the **Counter** GenServer with an initial value of 0.
- **opts** = [...]: This list specifies options for the supervisor.
  - **strategy: :one_for_one** means that if one child process crashes, only that process will be restarted.

- name: **MyApp.Supervisor** gives the supervisor a name, which can be useful for debugging and monitoring.
- **Supervisor.start_link(children, opts):** This starts the supervisor with the specified children and options.

Step 3: Run the Application

To run your application, you can use the following command in your terminal:

Bash

```
iex -S mix
```

This will start IEx (the interactive Elixir shell) with your application running in the background. You can then interact with your Counter GenServer as before:

Elixir

```
iex> Counter.value()
0
iex> Counter.increment()
:ok
iex> Counter.value()
1
```

Understanding the Structure

Congratulations! You've just built a basic OTP application. Let's recap the key components:

- **Application module (MyApp.Application):** The entry point and container for your application.

- **Supervisor:** A process that monitors and manages child processes.
- **Worker process (Counter GenServer):** Performs the actual work of the application.

Benefits of this Structure

This OTP structure provides several benefits:

- **Fault tolerance:** If the Counter process crashes, the supervisor will automatically restart it.
- **Organization:** It provides a clear structure for organizing your application's components.
- **Scalability:** You can easily add more worker processes to handle increased workload.

This is a basic example, but it demonstrates the fundamental principles of building OTP applications. As your applications grow in complexity, you can add more supervisors, worker processes, and other OTP components to create robust and scalable systems. So, keep experimenting, and let OTP guide you in building reliable and maintainable Elixir applications!

4.4 Testing with ExUnit

Testing is a crucial part of software development, and Elixir provides a fantastic built-in testing framework called ExUnit. Think of ExUnit as your quality assurance team, helping you ensure that your code behaves as expected and catches any bugs before they sneak into production.

Why Test?

Testing provides numerous benefits:

- **Confidence:** Tests give you confidence that your code works correctly.
- **Bug Prevention:** Tests help you catch bugs early in the development process, making them easier and cheaper to fix.
- **Documentation:** Tests serve as living documentation of your code, showing how it's supposed to be used.
- **Refactoring Safety Net:** When you refactor your code, tests act as a safety net, ensuring that you haven't introduced any regressions.

Getting Started with ExUnit

ExUnit is built into Elixir, so you don't need to install anything extra. Let's write a simple test for our Counter GenServer from the previous section.

Step 1: Create a Test File

By convention, test files in Elixir have the .exs extension and are placed in the test directory of your project. Let's create a file named test/counter_test.exs.

Step 2: Define the Test Module

Inside the test file, we'll define a test module:

Elixir

```elixir
defmodule CounterTest do
use ExUnit.Case
# ... (Tests will go here) ...
end
```

We use the **use ExUnit.Case** macro to include ExUnit's testing functionality.

Step 3: Write a Test Case

Now, let's write a test case to verify that our Counter GenServer works correctly:

Elixir

```
test "incrementing the counter" do
{:ok, pid} = Counter.start_link(0)
assert Counter.value() == 0
Counter.increment()
assert Counter.value() == 1
end
```

Let's break down this test case:

- **test "incrementing the counter" do ... end**: This defines a test case with a descriptive name.
- **{:ok, pid} = Counter.start_link(0)**: We start the Counter GenServer with an initial value of 0.
- **assert Counter.value() == 0**: We use the **assert** macro to check that the initial value of the counter is indeed 0.
- **Counter.increment()**: We increment the counter.
- **assert Counter.value() == 1**: We assert that the counter value is now 1.

Step 4: Run the Tests

To run your tests, use the following command in your terminal:

```
mix test
```

ExUnit will execute your test cases and report the results. If all tests pass, you'll see a green output. If any test fails, ExUnit will provide detailed information about the failure, helping you pinpoint the issue.

Assertions and Other ExUnit Features

ExUnit provides a variety of assertion macros to help you test different conditions:

- **assert**: Checks that an expression evaluates to true.
- **refute**: Checks that an expression evaluates to false.
- **assert_equal**: Checks that two values are equal.
- **assert_match**: Checks that a value matches a pattern.
- **assert_raise**: Checks that an expression raises a specific exception.

ExUnit also provides features like:

- **setup blocks:** For setting up test data or initial conditions before each test.
- **describe blocks:** For grouping related test cases.
- **Asynchronous testing:** For testing asynchronous operations.

Testing Best Practices

Here are a few tips for writing effective tests:

- **Test small units:** Focus on testing individual functions or modules in isolation.

- **Write clear and descriptive test names:** Make it easy to understand what each test case is verifying.
- **Use assertions to check expected outcomes:** Don't rely on manual inspection of test output.
- **Keep your tests fast:** Fast tests provide quicker feedback and encourage more frequent testing.

ExUnit is a powerful tool for ensuring the quality and reliability of your Elixir code. By embracing testing and incorporating it into your development workflow, you can build robust and maintainable applications with confidence. So, write those tests, run them regularly, and let ExUnit be your guide in creating high-quality Elixir code!

Chapter 5: Phoenix Framework Fundamentals

Let's dive into the exciting world of Phoenix, Elixir's powerful web framework! Phoenix makes it a breeze to build high-performance, scalable web applications. Think of it as your toolkit for crafting dynamic websites, APIs, and real-time applications with ease. In this chapter, we'll explore the fundamental concepts of Phoenix, including its MVC architecture, routing, controllers, views, templates, and the magic of plugs.

5.1 Introduction to Phoenix

Okay, let's get acquainted with Phoenix, Elixir's awesome web framework! Phoenix is like your supercharged toolkit for building dynamic, high-performance web applications. It takes the strengths of Elixir, like concurrency, fault-tolerance, and functional programming, and combines them with a productive and enjoyable development experience.

Why Choose Phoenix?

You might be wondering, "Why should I use Phoenix? There are so many other web frameworks out there!" Well, here are a few reasons why Phoenix stands out:

- **Blazing Fast and Scalable:** Phoenix applications are renowned for their speed and ability to handle a huge number of concurrent users. This is thanks to Elixir's concurrency model, which leverages the Erlang VM (BEAM) to efficiently manage many processes.

- **Developer Productivity:** Phoenix provides a well-organized structure, clear conventions, and helpful generators that accelerate development. It's like having a blueprint and a set of power tools to help you build your web app quickly and efficiently.
- **Real-time Features Made Easy:** Phoenix offers LiveView, a powerful feature that allows you to build real-time, interactive elements without writing tons of client-side JavaScript. It's like magic!
- **Enjoyable Development Experience:** Phoenix embraces Elixir's elegant syntax and functional paradigm, making it a joy to work with. You'll find yourself writing clean, maintainable code that's easy to understand and reason about.

Key Features of Phoenix

Let's take a closer look at some of the key features that make Phoenix so powerful:

- **MVC Architecture:** Phoenix follows the Model-View-Controller pattern, providing a clear separation of concerns. This helps you organize your code and makes it easier to maintain and test.
- **Powerful Routing:** Phoenix has a robust routing system that maps incoming requests to the appropriate controller actions. You can define routes based on HTTP verbs (GET, POST, PUT, DELETE), URL patterns, and other criteria.

- **Controllers:** Controllers are modules that handle requests, interact with models to fetch or update data, and prepare data for the view.
- **Views:** Views are responsible for rendering templates and presenting data to the user.
- **Templates:** Templates define the structure and content of your web pages. Phoenix uses EEx (Embedded Elixir), a templating language that allows you to embed Elixir code within HTML.
- **Plugs:** Plugs are modular components that can be plugged into the request pipeline to perform tasks like authentication, logging, or data transformation.

Creating a Phoenix Project

Let's get our hands dirty and create a simple Phoenix project!

1. **Install the Phoenix archive:** If you haven't already, you'll need to install the Phoenix archive. You can do this using the following command in your terminal:

Bash

```
mix archive.install hex phx_new
```

2. **Create a new project:** Use the mix phx.new command to create a new Phoenix project:

Bash

```
mix phx.new my_app
```

(Replace **my_app** with your desired project name.)

3. **Follow the instructions:** The **phx.new** command will provide instructions for installing dependencies and starting the server.
4. **Start the server:** Once the dependencies are installed, you can start the Phoenix server:

Bash

```
cd my_app
mix phx.server
```

Now, open your web browser and visit http://localhost:4000. You should see the default Phoenix welcome page!

This was just a quick introduction to Phoenix. In the following sections, we'll delve deeper into its various components and learn how to build dynamic and interactive web applications. So, get excited, and let's explore the power of Phoenix!

5.2 MVC Architecture in Phoenix

Let's explore how Phoenix organizes your web application using the Model-View-Controller (MVC) architectural pattern! MVC is a popular way to structure web applications, and Phoenix embraces it to provide a clear separation of concerns and make your code more organized, maintainable, and testable.

Understanding MVC

Think of MVC like a well-coordinated team working together to create a delicious meal:

- **Model (The Chef):** The model represents the data and the "ingredients" of your application. It's responsible for fetching data from databases, performing calculations, enforcing business rules, and generally managing the core logic of your app.
- **View (The Waiter):** The view is responsible for "presenting" the data to the user. It takes the prepared data from the controller and "serves" it up in a visually appealing way, usually as HTML.
- **Controller (The Maître d'):** The controller acts as the intermediary between the model and the view. It receives "orders" (requests) from the user, interacts with the "chef" (model) to get the necessary data, and then instructs the "waiter" (view) on how to present it.

MVC in Phoenix

Let's see how this translates to a Phoenix application:

- **Model:** In Phoenix, models often interact with databases using Ecto (which we'll explore in the next chapter). They define the structure of your data and provide functions for accessing and manipulating it.
- **View:** Views in Phoenix render templates. Templates are files (usually written in EEx, Embedded Elixir)

that define the structure and content of your web pages.

- **Controller:** Controllers receive requests from the user, interact with models to fetch or update data, and then pass that data to the view for rendering.

Benefits of MVC

- **Organization:** MVC helps you organize your code by separating different concerns. This makes it easier to find and modify specific parts of your application.
- **Maintainability:** Clear separation makes it easier to maintain and update your code over time. Changes in one part of the application are less likely to affect other parts.
- **Testability:** MVC makes it easier to test your code by isolating different components. You can test models, views, and controllers independently.
- **Reusability:** You can reuse models and views across different parts of your application.

Example: A Simple Blog

Let's imagine you're building a simple blog application. Here's how MVC might come into play:

- **Model (Post):** Represents a blog post with fields like title, content, and author. It might have functions to fetch posts from the database, create new posts, or update existing ones.
- **View (PostView):** Renders templates to display blog posts, such as a list of posts on the index page or a single post on a show page.

- **Controller (`PostController`):** Handles requests related to blog posts, such as displaying a list of posts (`index` action), showing a single post (`show` action), creating a new post (`create` action), and so on.

Code Example (Simplified)

Elixir

```elixir
# Model (Post)
defmodule MyApp.Post do
# ... (Code to interact with the database) ...
end

# View (PostView)
defmodule MyAppWeb.PostView do
use MyAppWeb, :view
end

# Controller (PostController)
defmodule MyAppWeb.PostController do
use MyAppWeb, :controller

def index(conn, _params) do
posts = MyApp.Post.all() # Fetch posts from the model
render(conn, "index.html", posts: posts) # Pass posts to
the view
end
end
```

This is a simplified example, but it illustrates how the model, view, and controller work together in a Phoenix application.

By understanding the MVC pattern and how it's implemented in Phoenix, you can build well-structured, maintainable, and scalable web applications. So, embrace MVC, and let it guide you in creating organized and efficient Phoenix projects!

5.3 Routing and Controllers

Alright, let's explore how Phoenix handles incoming requests and directs them to the appropriate parts of your application! This involves two key components: routing and controllers. Think of routing as the traffic cop of your web application, directing incoming requests to the right destination. Controllers, on the other hand, are like the offices where the actual work gets done.

Routing:

Routing is the process of mapping incoming requests to specific actions in your application. When a user visits a URL in their browser, Phoenix's router examines the request and determines which controller and action should handle it.

Defining Routes

Routes are defined in your Phoenix application's router.ex file. This file uses a clear and concise syntax to define how different URLs should be handled.

Let's look at an example:

Elixir

```
defmodule MyAppWeb.Router do
use MyAppWeb, :router
scope "/", MyAppWeb do
pipe_through :browser # Use the default browser stack
get "/", PageController, :index
get "/about", PageController, :about
post "/contact", ContactController, :create
end
end
```

This code defines three routes:

- get "/", PageController, :index: This maps a GET request to the root URL ("/") to the index action in the PageController.
- get "/about", PageController, :about: This maps a GET request to the "/about" URL to the about action in the PageController.
- post "/contact", ContactController, :create: This maps a POST request to the "/contact" URL to the create action in the ContactController.

As you can see, the routing syntax specifies the HTTP verb (GET, POST, etc.), the URL path, and the controller and action to handle the request.

Controllers:

Controllers are modules that contain functions called "actions." These actions are responsible for processing requests, interacting with models, and preparing data for the view.

Let's take a look at a simple controller:

Elixir

```
defmodule MyAppWeb.PageController do
use MyAppWeb, :controller
def index(conn, _params) do
render(conn, "index.html")
end
def about(conn, _params) do
render(conn, "about.html", page_title:[1] "About Us")
end
end
```

This **PageController** defines two actions:

- **index(conn, _params)**: This action handles requests to the root URL ("/"). It simply renders the index.html template.
- **about(conn, _params)**: This action handles requests to the "/about" URL. It renders the about.html template and passes a page_title assign to it.

The Connection (conn)

The conn argument in the controller actions represents the connection to the client. It contains information about the request, such as the HTTP method, headers, and parameters. You can use the conn to access this information, set cookies, and send responses.

Parameters (params)

The params argument contains any parameters that were sent with the request, such as query string parameters or form data.

Putting It Together

When a user visits your website, the following happens:

1. **Request:** The user's browser sends a request to your Phoenix application.
2. **Routing:** Phoenix's router examines the request and matches it to a route defined in **router.ex**.
3. **Controller:** The router dispatches the request to the appropriate controller action.
4. **Action:** The controller action processes the request, interacts with models if necessary, and prepares data.
5. **Response:** The controller action uses the **render** function to send a response to the user, usually by rendering a template.

Dynamic Routes

Phoenix also supports dynamic routes, where parts of the URL can be captured as parameters. For example:

Elixir

```
get "/posts/:id", PostController, :show
```

This route matches URLs like **/posts/1**, **/posts/2**, etc. The **:id** part is a dynamic segment, and its value will be captured and passed to the **show** action in the **PostController** as a parameter.

By understanding routing and controllers, you can effectively handle incoming requests and direct them to the appropriate parts of your Phoenix application. So, explore the routing syntax, experiment with controllers, and build dynamic web applications that respond to user interactions!

5.4 Views and Templates (EEx)

Alright, let's explore how Phoenix renders the content that users see in their browsers! This involves views and templates, two key components that work together to present data in a visually appealing way. Think of views as the "chefs" who prepare the data and templates as the "plates" that present it.

Templates: The Presentation Layer

Templates define the structure and content of your web pages. In Phoenix, templates are typically HTML files with the .html.eex extension. EEx stands for "Embedded Elixir," which means you can embed Elixir code directly within your HTML.

Here's a simple example of a template:

HTML

```
<!DOCTYPE html>
<html lang="en">
<head>
<meta charset="UTF-8">
<title>My Website</title>
</head>
<body>
<h1>Welcome to My Website!</h1>
<p>This is¹ the home page.</p>
</body>
</html>
```

This template defines a basic HTML page with a title, a heading, and a paragraph.

Views: Preparing the Data

Views are modules that act as intermediaries between controllers and templates. They are responsible for:

- **Preparing data:** Taking data from the controller and transforming it into a format suitable for the template.
- **Rendering templates:** Taking a template file and rendering it with the prepared data.

Here's an example of a view module:

Elixir

```elixir
defmodule MyAppWeb.PageView do
  use MyAppWeb, :view
end
```

This `PageView` module doesn't define any custom functions, so it will use the default rendering behavior provided by Phoenix.

Rendering Templates from Controllers

In your controller actions, you use the render function to render a template:

Elixir

```elixir
defmodule MyAppWeb.PageController do
  use MyAppWeb, :controller
```

```
def index(conn, _params) do
render(conn, "index.html")
end
end
```

This code renders the **index.html.eex** template located in the **templates/page** directory (by convention).

Passing Data to Templates

You can pass data from the controller to the template using assigns:

Elixir

```
defmodule MyAppWeb.PageController do
use MyAppWeb, :controller
def about(conn, _params) do
render(conn, "about.html", page_title: "About Us",
current_user: "Alice")
end
end
```

This code passes two assigns, **page_title** and **current_user**, to the **about.html.eex** template.

Using Assigns in Templates

You can access assigns in your templates using @:

HTML

```
<!DOCTYPE html>
<html lang="en">
<head>
```

```
<meta charset="UTF-8">
<title><%= @page_title %></title>
</head>
<body>
<h1><%= @page_title %></h1>
<p>Welcome, <%= @current_user %>!</p>
</body>
</html>
```

This template uses `<%= @page_title %>` to display the page title and `<%= @current_user %>` to display the current user's name.

EEx: Embedded Elixir

EEx allows you to embed Elixir code within your templates using different tags:

- `<%= ... %>`: Evaluates the Elixir expression and outputs the result.
- `<% ... %>`: Executes Elixir code without outputting anything.
- `<%# ... %>`: Comments out Elixir code.

Example with EEx

HTML

```
<ul>
<%= for item <- ["apple", "banana", "cherry"] do %>
<li><%= item %></li>
<% end %>
</ul>
```

This code uses a **for** loop to generate a **list** of fruits.

By understanding views and templates, you can effectively render dynamic content and create visually appealing web pages in your Phoenix applications. So, experiment with EEx, create dynamic templates, and bring your Phoenix applications to life!

5.5 Phoenix Endpoints and Plugs

Alright, let's take a look under the hood of Phoenix and explore how it processes incoming requests! This involves understanding endpoints and plugs, two essential components that work together to handle requests and prepare them for your controllers and views.

Endpoints:

Think of an endpoint as the "front door" of your Phoenix application. It's the first point of contact for all incoming requests. The endpoint is responsible for receiving requests, performing some initial processing, and then passing them through a pipeline of plugs.

Plugs:

Plugs are like modular building blocks that you can "plug" into the request pipeline to perform various tasks. They are functions that take a connection (conn) and return a modified connection. This allows you to compose complex request handling logic by combining simple, reusable plugs.

Common Uses of Plugs

Plugs can be used for a wide range of tasks, such as:

- **Authentication:** Verify user identity (e.g., checking for a valid session).
- **Authorization:** Check user permissions (e.g., ensuring a user has access to a specific resource).
- **Logging:** Record request information for debugging or analysis.
- **Parsing:** Parse request bodies (e.g., converting JSON data into Elixir maps).
- **Formatting:** Format responses (e.g., setting headers or encoding data).
- **Error Handling:** Handle errors and exceptions.

Defining Plugs

You can define your own plugs or use the many built-in plugs provided by Phoenix and other libraries. Here's an example of a simple plug that logs the request method and path:

Elixir

```
defmodule MyAppWeb.LogRequestPlug do
import Plug.Conn
def init(opts), do: opts
def call(conn, _opts) do
IO.puts("Received         request:        #{conn.method}
#{conn.request_path}")
conn
end
end
```

This **LogRequestPlug** uses **Plug.Conn** to access the request method and path and logs them to the console. It then returns the conn to continue the request processing.

Plug Pipeline

Phoenix uses a plug pipeline to process requests. The endpoint defines the initial pipeline, and you can add or remove plugs as needed. Each plug in the pipeline receives the connection, performs its task, and passes the modified connection to the next plug.

Example: Using Plugs in the Router

You can use plugs in your router to define pipelines for different groups of routes. Here's an example:

Elixir

```elixir
defmodule MyAppWeb.Router do
use MyAppWeb, :router
pipeline :browser do
plug :accepts, ["html"]
plug :fetch_session
plug :fetch_flash[1]
plug MyAppWeb.LogRequestPlug # Include our custom plug
end
scope "/", MyAppWeb do
pipe_through :browser
# ... your routes ...
end
end
```

This code defines a :browser pipeline that includes plugs to handle HTML acceptance, session fetching, flash messages, and our custom LogRequestPlug. All routes within the scope block will use this pipeline.

Benefits of Plugs

- **Modularity:** Plugs promote modularity by breaking down request handling into smaller, reusable units.
- **Flexibility:** You can easily add, remove, or reorder plugs in the pipeline to customize request processing.
- **Reusability:** You can reuse plugs across different parts of your application or even in different projects.

By understanding endpoints and plugs, you can gain deeper control over how Phoenix handles requests. You can customize the request pipeline, add custom logic, and build robust and maintainable web applications. So, explore the world of plugs, experiment with different combinations, and leverage their power to enhance your Phoenix applications!

Chapter 6: Persistence with Ecto

It's time to learn how to store and retrieve data in your Phoenix applications! This is where Ecto comes in. Ecto is Elixir's powerful database wrapper and query language. Think of it as your translator and guide for interacting with databases, making it a breeze to work with data in your applications.

6.1 Introduction to Ecto

Alright, let's explore Ecto, Elixir's powerful database wrapper and query language! Think of Ecto as your friendly guide and translator for interacting with databases. It makes working with data in your Elixir applications a breeze, whether you're using SQL databases like PostgreSQL and MySQL, or NoSQL databases like MongoDB.

Why Ecto?

You might be wondering, "Why bother with Ecto? Can't I just write raw SQL queries?" While you certainly can, Ecto offers several advantages that make it a compelling choice:

- **Productivity Booster:** Ecto simplifies database interactions, allowing you to focus on your application's logic rather than getting bogged down in database-specific details. It's like having a helpful assistant who handles the tedious parts, freeing you up to focus on the bigger picture.

- **Maintainability Champion:** Ecto encourages you to write clean, organized code that's easier to understand and maintain. This is especially important as your application grows and evolves.
- **Type Safety Superhero:** Ecto schemas provide compile-time checks, meaning the compiler can catch potential errors early in the development process, before they become bigger problems. It's like having a spellchecker for your database interactions.
- **Database Agnosticity:** Ecto can work with various databases, giving you flexibility and making it easier to switch databases if needed. It's like having a universal travel adapter for your data.

Key Features of Ecto

Let's take a closer look at some of the key features that make Ecto so powerful:

- **Schemas:** Schemas define the structure of your data and how it maps to database tables. They're like blueprints that describe the shape and properties of your data.
- **Repositories:** Repositories provide an abstraction layer for interacting with the database. They offer functions for common operations like inserting, updating, and deleting data. Think of them as your database command center.
- **Queries:** Ecto allows you to construct database queries using Elixir's elegant syntax. This makes your queries more readable and easier to understand compared to raw SQL.

- **Changesets:** Changesets represent changes to your data and provide validation and error handling. They act as a safety net, ensuring that only valid data makes its way into your database.
- **Migrations:** Migrations help you manage database schema changes over time. As your application evolves and you need to add or modify tables or columns, migrations keep your database in sync.

Adding Ecto to Your Project

Let's add Ecto to your Phoenix project!

1. **Add the dependency:** In your mix.exs file, add ecto_sql and a database adapter (e.g., postgrex for PostgreSQL) to your dependencies:

Elixir

```
defp deps do

[

{:ecto_sql, "~> 3.0"},

{:postgrex, ">= 0.0.0"}

]

end
```

2. **Fetch the dependencies:** Run mix deps.get in your terminal to install the new dependencies.
3. **Configure your database:** In your config/config.exs file, configure your database connection:

Elixir

```
config :my_app, MyApp.Repo,

  database: "my_app_dev",

  username: "postgres",

  password: "postgres",

  hostname: "localhost",

  show_sensitive_data_on_connection_error: true
```

4. **Create your repository:** Create a repository module (e.g., **lib/my_app/repo.ex**) and define your repository:

Elixir

```
defmodule MyApp.Repo do

use Ecto.Repo,

otp_app: :my_app,

adapter: Ecto.Adapters.Postgres

end
```

Now, you have Ecto set up in your Phoenix project, and you're ready to start defining schemas, writing queries, and interacting with your database!

6.2 Defining Schemas and Migrations

Let's learn how to define the structure of your data and manage database changes with Ecto schemas and migrations! Think of schemas as blueprints that describe the shape and properties of your data, and migrations as the construction workers that build and modify your database tables.

Schemas:

Schemas in Ecto define the structure of your data and how it maps to database tables. They specify the fields (columns) in your tables, their data types, and any constraints or validations.

Defining a Schema

Let's create a schema for a User in our application:

Elixir

```elixir
defmodule MyApp.Accounts.User do

use Ecto.Schema

import Ecto.Changeset

schema "users" do

field :name, :string

field :email, :string

field :age, :integer

timestamps()
```

```
end

@doc false

def changeset(user, attrs) do

user

|> cast(attrs, [:name, :email, :age])

|> validate_required([:name, :email, :age])

end[1]

end
```

Let's break down this code:

- **use Ecto.Schema**: This line includes the Ecto.Schema
  module, providing the necessary functionality for
  defining schemas.
- **schema "users" do ... end**: This block defines the
  schema itself. The **"users"** string specifies the name
  of the database table that this schema maps to.
- **field :name, :string**: This defines a field named **name**
  with the data type :string.
- **timestamps()**: This macro adds two fields,
  inserted_at and **updated_at**, which automatically
  track when the record was created and updated.

Migrations:

Migrations are Elixir modules that describe how to modify your database schema. They are used to create new tables, add columns, modify existing columns, or drop tables.

Creating a Migration

To create a migration for our User schema, we can use the following command in our terminal:

Bash

```
mix ecto.gen.migration create_users
```

This will generate a migration file in the **priv/repo/migrations** directory. Open this file and add the following code:

Elixir

```
defmodule MyApp.Repo.Migrations.CreateUser do

use Ecto.Migration

def change do

create table(:users) do

add :name, :string

add :email, :string

add² :age, :integer

timestamps()

end
```

end

end[3]

This migration defines a **change** function that describes the changes to be made to the database. In this case, it creates a **users** table with the columns defined in our User schema.

Running Migrations

To apply the migration and create the **users** table in your database, run the following command:

Bash

mix ecto.migrate

Ecto will keep track of which migrations have been applied, so you can safely run this command multiple times without causing issues.

Rolling Back Migrations

If you need to undo a migration, you can use the following command:

Bash

mix ecto.rollback

This will revert the changes made by the last migration.

Why Migrations Matter

Migrations are essential for managing database schema changes over time. They provide several benefits:

- **Version Control:** Migrations provide a history of your database schema changes, making it easy to track how your database has evolved.
- **Reproducibility:** You can easily recreate your database schema on different environments (development, staging, production) by running the migrations.
- **Collaboration:** Migrations make it easier for teams to collaborate on database changes, ensuring that everyone's database is in sync.

By understanding schemas and migrations, you can effectively define the structure of your data and manage database changes in your Phoenix applications. So, create those schemas, write those migrations, and let Ecto handle the heavy lifting of database management!

6.3 Working with Repositories

Let's learn how to interact with your database using Ecto repositories! Think of repositories as your command center for database operations. They provide a convenient abstraction layer that simplifies common tasks like inserting, updating, deleting, and querying data.

What's a Repository?

A repository is a module that encapsulates the logic for accessing and manipulating data in your database. It acts as an intermediary between your application code and the database, providing a clean and organized way to perform database operations.

Benefits of Using Repositories

- **Abstraction:** Repositories abstract away the low-level details of database interactions, allowing you to focus on your application logic.
- **Centralized Logic:** They provide a central place to define your database access logic, making it easier to maintain and update.
- **Testability:** Repositories can be easily mocked or stubbed in tests, making it easier to test your application code in isolation.

Defining a Repository

You typically define a repository module in your Elixir application. Here's an example:

Elixir

```elixir
defmodule MyApp.Repo do

use Ecto.Repo,

otp_app: :my_app,

adapter: Ecto.Adapters.Postgres

end
```

This code defines a repository named MyApp.Repo that uses the PostgreSQL adapter. You'll need to configure your database connection in your config/config.exs file, as we discussed in the previous section.

Common Repository Functions

Ecto repositories provide a variety of functions for performing common database operations. Here are a few examples:

- **insert(struct)**: Inserts a new record into the database.

Elixir

```
user = %MyApp.Accounts.User{name: "Alice", email: "alice@example.com", age: 30}

{:ok, user} = MyApp.Repo.insert(user)
```

- get(schema, id): Retrieves a record by its ID.

Elixir

```
user = MyApp.Repo.get(MyApp.Accounts.User, 123)
```

- update(changeset): Updates an existing record.

Elixir

```
user = MyApp.Repo.get(MyApp.Accounts.User, 123)

changeset = MyApp.Accounts.User.changeset(user, %{name: "Bob"})

{:ok, user} = MyApp.Repo.update(changeset)
```

- delete(struct): Deletes a record.

Elixir

```elixir
user = MyApp.Repo.get(MyApp.Accounts.User, 123)

{:ok, user} = MyApp.Repo.delete(user)
```

- all(query): Executes a query and returns all matching records.

Elixir

```elixir
users = MyApp.Repo.all(from u in MyApp.Accounts.User,
where: u.age > 25)
```

Building Queries with Ecto

Ecto provides a powerful query language that allows you to construct database queries using Elixir's syntax. Here's an example:

Elixir

```elixir
query = from u in MyApp.Accounts.User,

where: u.age > 25,

select: u.name

users = MyApp.Repo.all(query)
```

This query selects the names of all users who are older than 25.

Ecto.Query

Ecto's query language is built on the Ecto.Query module, which provides a variety of functions for building queries. You can use functions like from, where, select, order_by, limit, and many more to construct complex queries.

Transactions

Ecto also supports transactions, which allow you to group multiple database operations into a single unit of work. This ensures that either all operations succeed or none of them do, maintaining data consistency.

Elixir

Ecto.Multi.new()

|> Ecto.Multi.insert(:user, user)

|> Ecto.Multi.insert(:post, post)

|> MyApp.Repo.transaction()

This code creates a transaction that inserts a user and a post.

By understanding repositories and Ecto's query language, you can effectively interact with your database and build data-driven applications in Elixir. So, explore the repository functions, experiment with queries, and leverage the power of Ecto to manage your data with ease!

6.4 Associations and Database Relationships

Alright, let's explore how to represent relationships between different data entities in your Elixir applications using Ecto associations! Think of associations as the connections between different pieces of your data, like the links in a chain or the threads in a web. They allow you to model real-world relationships, such as a user having many posts or a product belonging to a category.

Why Associations?

Associations provide several benefits:

- **Data Modeling:** They help you model real-world relationships between different entities in your application.
- **Data Integrity:** They enforce referential integrity, ensuring that relationships between records are valid.
- **Convenience:** They provide convenient functions for accessing related data, making it easier to work with your data.

Types of Associations

Ecto supports several types of associations to represent different kinds of relationships:

- **belongs_to:** Represents a one-to-one or many-to-one relationship. For example, a post *belongs to* a user, or a comment *belongs to* a post.

- **has_many**: Represents a one-to-many relationship. For example, a user *has many* posts, or a category *has many* products.
- **has_one**: Represents a one-to-one relationship where a record *has one* associated record. For example, a user *has one* profile.
- **many_to_many**: Represents a many-to-many relationship. For example, a post can have *many* tags, and a tag can belong to *many* posts.

Defining Associations

Let's see how to define associations in your Ecto schemas.

Example: belongs_to and has_many

Elixir

```
# lib/my_app/accounts/user.ex

defmodule MyApp.Accounts.User do

use Ecto.Schema

import Ecto.Changeset

 schema "users" do

field :name, :string

 field :email, :string

has_many :posts, MyApp.Blog.Post

timestamps()

end
```

```
# ... changeset ...

end

# lib/my_app/blog/post.ex

defmodule MyApp.Blog.Post do

use Ecto.Schem

import Ecto.Changeset

schema "posts" do

field :title, :string

field :content, :text

belongs_to :user, MyApp.Accounts.User

timestamps()

 end

# ... changeset ...

end
```

In this example, we have two schemas, User and Post.

- The User schema has a **has_many** :posts, MyApp.Blog.Post association, indicating that a user can have many posts.
- The **Post** schema has a **belongs_to** :user, **MyApp.Accounts.User** association, indicating that a post belongs to a user.

Working with Associations

Once you've defined associations, Ecto provides convenient functions for accessing related data.

- **Preloading:** You can preload associated data using the preload function in your queries. This avoids the "N+1 query problem" by fetching related data in a single query.

Elixir

```
users = MyApp.Repo.all(from u in MyApp.Accounts.User, preload: [:posts])
```

This query fetches all users and their associated posts in a single query.

- **Accessing Associated Data:** You can access associated data using dot notation.

Elixir

```
user = MyApp.Repo.get(MyApp.Accounts.User, 123)

user.posts # Access the user's posts
```

- **Building Queries with Associations:** You can use associations in your queries to filter or order data based on related records.

Elixir

```
posts = MyApp.Repo.all(from p in MyApp.Blog.Post,
where: p.user_id == 123)
```

This query fetches all posts that belong to the user with ID 123.

Foreign Keys

Ecto automatically manages foreign keys for you based on the associations you define. In the example above, a user_id column will be added to the posts table to represent the relationship between posts and users.

Database Relationships

Ecto associations map to different types of database relationships:

- **One-to-One:** A record in one table is associated with at most one record in another table.
- **One-to-Many:** A record in one table can be associated with multiple records in another table.
- **Many-to-Many:** Records in one table can be associated with multiple records in another table, and vice versa.[1]

By understanding associations and how they relate to database relationships, you can effectively model and work with complex data structures in your Elixir applications. So, define those associations, preload your data, and let Ecto handle the complexities of database relationships for you!

6.5 Changesets and Validations

Think of changesets as a staging area for your data, where you can apply changes, validate them, and handle any errors before saving the data to the database. Validations are like the quality control checks that ensure your data meets the required standards.

Why Changesets?

Changesets provide several benefits:

- **Data Integrity:** They help you maintain data integrity by enforcing validation rules and preventing invalid data from being saved to the database.
- **Error Handling:** They provide a structured way to handle validation errors, allowing you to provide informative feedback to users.
- **Atomic Changes:** They represent changes as a single unit, ensuring that either all changes are applied or none of them are.

Creating Changesets

You typically create a changeset within your schema module. Here's an example:

Elixir

```elixir
defmodule MyApp.Accounts.User do

use Ecto.Schema

import Ecto.Changeset

  schema "users" do
```

```
field :name, :string

field :email, :string

field :age, :integer

timestamps()

end


def changeset(user, attrs) do

user

|> cast(attrs, [:name, :email, :age])

|> validate_required([:name, :email])[1]

|> validate_format(:email, ~r/@/)

|> validate_number(:age, greater_than_or_equal_to: 18)

 end

end
```

This code defines a **changeset** function that takes a **user** struct and a map of attributes (attrs) as input. It then performs the following steps:

1. **cast(attrs, [:name, :email, :age]):** This casts the attributes to the **user** struct, allowing changes to the **name, email,** and **age** fields.
2. **validate_required([:name, :email]):** This validates that the **name** and **email** fields are present.

3. **validate_format(:email, ~r/@/)**: This validates that the email field has a valid format (contains an "@" symbol).
4. **validate_number(:age, greater_than_or_equal_to: 18)**: This validates that the age is a number greater than or equal to 18.

Applying Changesets

Once you have a changeset, you can apply it to the database using the repository.

Elixir

```
# In your controller or other module

user = MyApp.Repo.get(MyApp.Accounts.User, 123)

changeset = MyApp.Accounts.User.changeset(user, %{name: "Bob"})

case MyApp.Repo.update(changeset) do

{:ok, user} ->

# Success! The user was updated.

{:error, changeset} ->

# Handle the errors

end
```

Handling Validation Errors

If the changeset is invalid, the Repo.update function will return {:error, changeset}. You can then access the errors using the errors function.

{:error, changeset} ->

errors = errors_on(changeset)

Display the errors to the user

Types of Validations

Ecto provides a variety of validation functions, including:

- **validate_required**: Ensures that a field is present.
- **validate_length**: Validates the length of a string.
- **validate_format**: Checks that a field matches a specific format (using a regular expression).
- **validate_number**: Validates a number field (e.g., greater than, less than, equal to).
- **validate_inclusion**: Checks that a value is included in a given list.
- **validate_exclusion**: Checks that a value is not included in a given list.
- **validate_acceptance**: Ensures that a boolean field is true (e.g., for terms of service agreement).

Custom Validations

You can also define your own custom validation functions to enforce specific rules.

Changeset Pipeline

The changeset functions are applied in a pipeline, similar to plugs. Each function receives the changeset, performs its validation, and returns the modified changeset.

By understanding changesets and validations, you can ensure that your Elixir applications handle data with integrity and provide a good user experience. So, define those changesets, add those validations, and let Ecto help you keep your data clean and consistent!

Chapter 7: Building APIs with Phoenix

Let's learn how to build APIs (Application Programming Interfaces) with Phoenix! APIs allow different applications to talk to each other and exchange data, like a universal language for software. Think of them as waiters taking orders from customers (other applications) and delivering food (data) from the kitchen (your application). Phoenix makes it easy to create robust and efficient APIs that can serve data to web applications, mobile apps, or other backend systems.

7.1 JSON Encoding and Decoding with Poison

Alright, let's learn how to work with JSON in your Phoenix APIs! JSON (JavaScript Object Notation) is like the universal language of APIs. It's a lightweight and human-readable format for exchanging data between applications. Think of it as a simple way to package information so that different applications can understand it, regardless of their programming language.

JSON is widely used in APIs for several reasons:

- **Simplicity:** It's easy to read and write, both for humans and machines.
- **Lightweight:** It's compact and efficient, making it ideal for transmitting data over networks.

- **Ubiquitous Support:** Almost every programming language has libraries for working with JSON.

Poison:

Phoenix uses the Poison library to handle JSON encoding and decoding. Poison is like your friendly librarian who helps you translate between Elixir data structures and JSON strings.

Encoding: From Elixir to JSON

To encode Elixir data structures (like maps, lists, and structs) into JSON strings, you can use the **Poison.encode!** function.

Elixir

iex> data = %{name: "Alice", age: 30, city: "Wonderland"}

%{age: 30, city: "Wonderland", name: "Alice"}

iex> Poison.encode!(data)

"{\"name\":\"Alice\",\"age\":30,\"city\":\"Wonderland\"}"

In this example, we have a map with information about Alice. Poison.encode! takes this map and converts it into a JSON string. As you can see, the keys and values are enclosed in double quotes, and the key-value pairs are separated by colons.

Decoding: From JSON to Elixir

To decode JSON strings back into Elixir data structures, you can use the **Poison.decode!** function.

Elixir

```
iex>                    json_string                    =
"{\"name\":\"Bob\",\"age\":25,\"city\":\"Exampleville\"
}"

"{\"name\":\"Bob\",\"age\":25,\"city\":\"Exampleville\"
}"

iex> Poison.decode!(json_string)

%{"name" => "Bob", "age" => 25, "city" =>
"Exampleville"}
```

Here, we have a JSON string representing information about Bob. **Poison.decode!** takes this string and converts it back into an Elixir map.

Handling Errors

Both **Poison.encode!** and **Poison.decode!** raise an error if they encounter invalid input. You can use **try...rescue** blocks to handle these errors gracefully.

Elixir

```
try do

Poison.decode!("")

rescue

Poison.Error -> "Invalid JSON string"
```

end

Using Poison in Your Phoenix API

You'll typically use Poison in your Phoenix controllers to encode data for responses and decode data from requests.

Elixir

```elixir
# In your controller

def index(conn, _params) do

users = MyApp.Accounts.list_users()

json = Poison.encode!(users)

conn

|> put_resp_content_type("application/json")

|> send_resp(200, json)

end
```

This code fetches a list of users, encodes it into JSON, sets the response content type to **application/json**, and sends the JSON response.

Beyond the Basics

Poison provides additional options for customizing encoding and decoding, such as handling different date formats or converting keys to atoms. You can explore these options in the Poison documentation.

By understanding JSON encoding and decoding with Poison, you can effectively handle data in your Phoenix APIs and communicate with other applications seamlessly. So, encode that data, decode those responses, and let Poison be your guide in the world of JSON!

7.2 RESTful API Design Principles

Let's dive into the world of RESTful API design! REST (Representational State Transfer) is like a set of guidelines or best practices for creating APIs that are easy to use, scalable, and maintainable. Think of it as a common language that helps different applications understand and communicate with each other effectively.

Why REST?

REST has become the dominant style for designing web APIs because it offers several benefits:

- **Simplicity:** RESTful APIs leverage the existing infrastructure of the web (HTTP) and use standard methods and status codes, making them easy to understand and work with.
- **Scalability:** RESTful APIs are stateless, meaning each request contains all the information needed to process it. This makes it easier to scale your API to handle a large number of requests.
- **Flexibility:** RESTful APIs can be used with various data formats, including JSON, XML, and HTML.

- **Evolution:** RESTful APIs can evolve over time without breaking existing clients, as long as you follow certain principles.

Key Principles of REST

Let's explore the key principles that guide RESTful API design:

1. **Client-Server Architecture:** RESTful APIs separate the client (the application consuming the API) from the server (the application providing the API). This separation allows for independent evolution and scalability of both client and server. Think of it like a restaurant where the customer (client) places an order (request) and the kitchen (server) prepares the food (data) without needing to know the customer's dietary preferences or allergies.

2. **Statelessness:** Each request from the client to the server must contain all the information necessary to understand and process the request. The server[1] should not store any client context between requests. This makes the API more scalable and reliable since the server doesn't need to maintain session state. It's like ordering food at a restaurant – each order is complete and independent, and the waiter doesn't need to remember your previous orders.

3. **Cacheability:** Responses from the server should explicitly state whether they can be cached or not. This allows clients (or intermediary servers) to cache responses, reducing the number of requests to the server and improving performance. It's like a restaurant offering a daily special that doesn't change

– the customer can "cache" that information and doesn't need to ask for the menu every time.

4. **Uniform Interface:** RESTful APIs define a consistent interface for interacting with resources. This involves using standard HTTP methods (GET, POST, PUT, DELETE) and URLs to represent resources. This consistency makes it easier for developers to understand and use your API. It's like a restaurant having a menu with clear categories and descriptions of the dishes.

5. **Layered System:** REST allows for the use of intermediary components (like load balancers, caches, or security layers) between the client and the server. These components can improve performance, scalability, and security without the client or server needing to be aware of them. Think of it like a restaurant having a host who greets customers and guides them to their tables, or a busboy who clears the tables, without the chef or customer needing to be involved.

6. **Code on Demand (Optional):** This principle allows the server to send executable code (like JavaScript) to the client. This is often used to provide client-side functionality or enhance the user interface. It's like a restaurant providing a tablet for customers to place orders or provide feedback.

RESTful Resources

In REST, you model your data as resources, which are identified by URLs. For example:

- /users: Represents a collection of users.

- **/users/123**: Represents a specific user with ID 123.

HTTP Methods

RESTful APIs use standard HTTP methods to perform operations on resources:

- **GET:** Retrieve a resource or a collection of resources.[2]
- **POST:** Create a new resource.
- **PUT:** Update an existing resource.
- **DELETE:** Delete a resource.[3]

Status Codes

RESTful APIs use HTTP status codes to indicate the outcome of a request:

- **200 OK:** The request was successful.
- **201 Created:** A new resource was created.
- **400 Bad Request:** The request was invalid.
- **404 Not Found:** The requested resource was not found.
- **500 Internal Server Error:** An error occurred on the server.

By following these RESTful API design principles, you can create APIs that are consistent, scalable, and easy to use. So, embrace REST, design your resources, choose the right HTTP methods, and build APIs that developers will love!

7.3 Authentication and Authorization

When building APIs, it's crucial to ensure that only authorized users or applications can access your valuable data. This involves two key concepts: authentication and authorization. Think of authentication as verifying someone's identity (like checking their ID card) and authorization as checking if they have permission to enter a specific room (access a resource).

Authentication:

Authentication is the process of verifying the identity of the user or application making a request to your API. It's like a bouncer at a club checking your ID to make sure you're old enough to enter.

Common Authentication Methods

There are several common ways to authenticate API requests:

- **API Keys:** Each user or application is assigned a unique API key, which they include in their requests. This is like a secret password that grants them access.
- **Basic Authentication:** The user provides their username and password with each request. This information is usually encoded using Base64 to prevent it from being sent in plain text.
- **OAuth 2.0:** This is a popular authorization framework that allows users to grant third-party applications access to their resources without sharing their credentials.[1] It's like giving someone a key to your house while you're away, but only allowing them to access certain rooms.
- **JWT (JSON Web Tokens):** JWTs are a compact and self-contained way to securely transmit information between parties as a JSON object.[2] They can be used to

represent claims, such as user identity or permissions.

Implementing Authentication in Phoenix

Phoenix provides various libraries and tools to help you implement authentication. Here's a simplified example using Guardian, a popular authentication library:

1. **Add Guardian to your project:**

Bash

```
mix deps.get guardian
```

2. **Configure Guardian:**

Elixir

```
# config/config.exs

config :my_app, MyAppWeb.Guardian,

issuer: "MyApp",

secret_key: "your_secret_key", # Replace with a strong secret key

 token_type: "access"
```

3. **Create a pipeline for protected routes:**

Elixir

```elixir
# lib/my_app_web/router.ex

pipeline :api_protected do

plug MyAppWeb.Guardian.Pipeline

plug :load_current_user

end

scope "/api", MyAppWeb do

pipe_through :api_protected

# ... your protected API routes ...

end
```

4. **Implement the** load_current_user **plug:**

Elixir

```elixir
# lib/my_app_web/plugs/load_current_user.ex

defmodule MyAppWeb.LoadCurrentUser do

import Plug.Conn

 alias MyAppWeb.Guardian

 def init(opts), do: opts

def call(conn, _opts) do

case Guardian.Plug.current_resource(conn) do
```

```
nil -> conn

user -> assign(conn, :current_user, user)

end

end

end
```

5. **Protect your controller actions:**

Elixir

```elixir
# lib/my_app_web/controllers/api_controller.ex

defmodule MyAppWeb.ApiController do

use MyAppWeb, :controller

def action(conn, _params) do

user = conn.assigns.current_user

# ... your action logic ...

end

end
```

Authorization: What Are You Allowed to Do?

Authorization is the process of determining what actions an authenticated user or application is allowed to perform. It's like checking if you have the key to a specific room in a building.

Authorization Strategies

- **Role-Based Access Control (RBAC):** Assign users to roles (e.g., admin, editor, viewer) and grant permissions based on those roles.
- **Access Control Lists (ACLs):** Define specific permissions for each user or group of users.
- **Policy-Based Authorization:** Define policies that determine access based on various factors, such as user attributes, resource attributes, and environmental conditions.

Implementing Authorization in Phoenix

You can implement authorization in your Phoenix controllers by checking the current_user and their permissions:

Elixir

```
def update_post(conn, %{"id" => id} = params) do

post = MyApp.Blog.get_post!(id)

if MyApp.Blog.can_update_post?(conn.assigns.current_user, post) do

# ... update the post ...

else
```

```
send_resp(conn, 403, "Forbidden")
```

```
end
```

```
end
```

By combining authentication and authorization, you can build secure APIs that protect your valuable data and ensure that only authorized users can access and modify it. So, implement those authentication mechanisms, define your authorization rules, and build APIs that are both functional and secure!

7.4 API Documentation and Testing

Alright, let's talk about API documentation and testing! Imagine you're cooking a delicious dish and want to share it with others. You'd probably provide a recipe, right? Well, API documentation is like a recipe for your API. It tells other developers how to use your API, what ingredients (data) to provide, and what to expect in return. Testing, on the other hand, is like tasting your dish to make sure it's cooked properly and tastes good.

Why API Documentation Matters

Good API documentation is essential for developers who will be using your API. It should be clear, concise, and easy to navigate. Here's why it's so important:

- **Usability:** Clear documentation makes it easier for developers to understand how to use your API, saving them time and frustration.

- **Adoption:** Well-documented APIs are more likely to be adopted by developers, as they can quickly understand its capabilities and integrate it into their applications.
- **Maintainability:** Documentation helps you keep track of your API's functionality and makes it easier to maintain and update over time.
- **Collaboration:** Documentation facilitates collaboration among developers working on the API, ensuring everyone is on the same page.

Documentation Tools

There are several tools available to help you document your APIs:

- **Swagger (OpenAPI):** Swagger is a popular open-source framework for designing, building, documenting, and consuming RESTful APIs. It provides a standardized way to describe your API using a YAML or JSON file, which can then be used to generate interactive documentation.
- **Postman:** Postman is a popular API platform that allows you to design, build, test, and document APIs. It provides a user-friendly interface for making API requests, viewing responses, and creating documentation.

Documenting Your Phoenix API with Swagger

Here's a simplified example of how to document your Phoenix API with Swagger:

1. **Add the phoenix_swagger dependency:**

Elixir

```elixir
# mix.exs

defp deps do

[

{:phoenix_swagger, "~> 0.10"}

]

end
```

2. **Configure Swagger:**

Elixir

```elixir
# config/config.exs

config :phoenix_swagger,

api_version: "1.0",

base_path: "/api",

swagger_version: "2.0",

info: %{

title: "My API",

description: "API documentation for my awesome application"

}
```

3. Annotate your controllers and schemas:

Elixir

```elixir
defmodule MyAppWeb.UserController do

use MyAppWeb, :controller

swagger_path :index do

get "/users"

summary "List all users"

description "Returns a list of all users"

produces "application/json"

response 200, "OK", Schema.ref(:User)

end

def index(conn, _params) do

# ...

end

end


defmodule MyApp.Accounts.User do

use Ecto.Schema
```

```
import Ecto.Changeset

@derive {PhoenixSwagger.Schema, title: "User"}

schema "users" do

field :name, :string, required: true

field :email, :string, required: true

timestamps()

end

# ...

end
```

4. **Generate the Swagger JSON:**

Bash

```
mix phoenix_swagger.generate
```

This will generate a **swagger.json** file in your **priv/static** directory.

5. **Access the Swagger UI:**

Phoenix Swagger provides a default UI for viewing your API documentation. You can access it by visiting **/api/swagger** in your browser.

API Testing:

Testing your API is crucial to ensure that it functions correctly and meets the needs of its consumers. Here are some common types of API tests:

- **Unit Tests:** Test individual functions or modules in isolation.
- **Integration Tests:** Test the interaction between different components of your API.
- **End-to-End Tests:** Test the entire API flow from the client's perspective.
- **Contract Tests:** Verify that your API adheres to a defined contract (e.g., a Swagger specification).
- **Performance Tests:** Measure the performance and scalability of your API.

Testing Tools

- **Postman:** Postman can be used for both manual and automated API testing.
- **ExUnit:** Elixir's built-in testing framework can be used to write automated API tests.

Example API Test with ExUnit

Elixir

```elixir
defmodule MyAppWeb.UserControllerTest do

use MyAppWeb.ConnCase

test "list users", %{conn: conn} do

conn = get(conn, "/api/users")

assert json_response(conn, 200)["data"] == []
```

end

end

By documenting and testing your API thoroughly, you can ensure that it's easy to use, reliable, and meets the needs of its consumers. So, write that documentation, create those tests, and build APIs that developers will love!

Chapter 8: Real-time Applications with Phoenix Channels

Get ready to supercharge your Phoenix applications with real-time features! In this chapter, we'll explore Phoenix Channels, a powerful tool for building interactive, real-time experiences. Think live chat, collaborative tools, online games, and more – all without the complexity of managing WebSockets directly.

8.1 WebSockets and Phoenix Channels

The world of real-time communication with WebSockets and Phoenix Channels! Imagine you're having a conversation with a friend. In a traditional web application, it would be like sending a letter back and forth - you write something, send it, wait for a reply, and so on. But with WebSockets, it's like having a live phone call where you can both talk and listen simultaneously.

WebSockets:

WebSockets provide a way to establish a persistent, bi-directional connection between a client (like a web browser) and a server. This allows for real-time data flow in both directions, making it perfect for applications that require instant updates, such as chat applications, collaborative tools, online games, and more.

WebSockets offer several advantages over traditional HTTP requests:

- **Real-time Communication:** Data can be sent and received instantly, without the delays of the request-response cycle.
- **Efficiency:** WebSockets reduce overhead by maintaining a single connection, unlike HTTP which requires a new connection for each request.
- **Bi-directional Communication:** Both the client and the server can send data at any time, enabling true real-time interactions.

Phoenix Channels:

While WebSockets are powerful, working with them directly can be a bit complex. This is where Phoenix Channels come in! Phoenix Channels provide a high-level abstraction on top of WebSockets, making it easier to build real-time features in your Elixir applications.

Think of Phoenix Channels as organized "chat rooms" within your application. Clients can join these channels and communicate with each other and the server in real-time.

Benefits of Phoenix Channels

- **Simplicity:** Channels hide the complexities of WebSockets, allowing you to focus on your application logic.
- **Scalability:** Phoenix Channels are designed to handle a large number of concurrent connections, making them suitable for real-time applications with many users.
- **Organization:** Channels provide a structured way to manage real-time communication, making your code cleaner and easier to maintain.

- **Flexibility:** You can easily broadcast messages to all clients in a channel or send private messages to specific clients.

Creating a Phoenix Channel

Let's create a simple Phoenix Channel:

1. **Generate the channel:** Use the following command in your terminal to generate a new channel:

Bash

```
mix phx.gen.channel Room
```

This will create a **RoomChannel** module in **lib/my_app_web/channels/room_channel.ex** and a JavaScript file in **assets/js/channels/room_channel.js**.

2. **Define the channel logic:**

Elixir

```
# lib/my_app_web/channels/room_channel.ex

defmodule MyAppWeb.RoomChannel do

use Phoenix.Channel

def join("room:lobby", _params, socket) do

{:ok, socket}

end
```

```elixir
def handle_in("shout", %{"message" => message},
socket) do

broadcast! socket, "shout", %{message: message}

{:noreply, socket}

end

end
```

This code defines a **RoomChannel** with two functions:

- **join/3**: Allows clients to join the "room:lobby" channel.
- **handle_in/3**: Handles incoming "shout" messages by broadcasting them to all clients in the channel.

3. **Connect to the channel from the client:**

JavaScript

```javascript
// assets/js/channels/room_channel.js

import {Socket} from "phoenix"

let socket = new Socket("/socket", {params: {token: window.userToken}})

socket.connect()

let channel = socket.channel("room:lobby",[1] {})

channel.join()
```

```
.receive("ok", resp => { console.log("Joined successfully",
resp) })
```

```
.receive("error", resp => { console.log("Unable to join",
resp)² })
```

```
channel.on("shout", payload => {
```

```
console.log("Received message:", payload.message)
```

```
})
```

This code connects to the Phoenix socket, joins the "room:lobby" channel, and listens for "shout" messages.

With this setup, you have a basic Phoenix Channel that can handle real-time communication between clients and the server. You can build upon this foundation to create various real-time features in your Phoenix applications. So, embrace the power of WebSockets and Phoenix Channels, and bring your applications to life with real-time interactivity!

8.2 Building a Chat Application

Let's put Phoenix Channels into action and build a real-time chat application! This will give you a hands-on understanding of how to use channels to create interactive features. Imagine building a virtual coffee shop where users can join, chat with each other, and see who's online. That's what we're going to create!

Step 1: Generate the Channel

First, let's generate a channel using the Phoenix generator:

Bash

```bash
mix phx.gen.channel Chat
```

This will create the necessary files for our chat channel:

- **lib/my_app_web/channels/chat_channel.ex**: This is where we'll define the server-side logic for our channel.
- **assets/js/channels/chat_channel.js**: This is where we'll write the client-side JavaScript code to interact with the channel.

Step 2: Define the Channel Logic

Open **lib/my_app_web/channels/chat_channel.ex** and update it with the following code:

Elixir

```elixir
defmodule MyAppWeb.ChatChannel do

use Phoenix.Channel

def join("chat:lobby", _params, socket) do

{:ok, socket}

end

def handle_in("new_msg", %{"body" => body}, socket) do

broadcast! socket, "new_msg", %{body: body, sender: socket.assigns.user_name}
```

```
{:noreply, socket}

end

end
```

This code defines a **ChatChannel** with two main functions:

- **join/3**: This function handles clients joining the "chat:lobby" channel. We'll assume for now that users are already authenticated and their username is available in **socket.assigns.user_name**.
- **handle_in/3**: This function handles incoming "new_msg" messages. It extracts the message body from the payload, adds the sender's username, and broadcasts the message to all clients in the channel using **broadcast!**.

Step 3: Implement Client-side JavaScript

Now, let's write the client-side JavaScript code to connect to the channel and handle sending and receiving messages. Open **assets/js/channels/chat_channel.js** and update it like this:

JavaScript

```javascript
import {Socket} from "phoenix"

let socket = new Socket("/socket", {params: {token: window.userToken}})

socket.connect()

let channel = socket.channel("chat:lobby",[1] {})
```

```
channel.join()

.receive("ok", resp => { console.log("Joined successfully",
resp) })

.receive("error", resp => { console.log("Unable to join",
resp) })

channel.on("new_msg",[2] payload[3] => {

let chatBox = document.querySelector("#chat-box")

let msg = `<p><strong>${payload.sender}:</strong>
${payload.body}</p>`

chatBox.innerHTML += msg

})


let                     messageInput                     =
document.querySelector("#message-input")

messageInput.addEventListener("keypress", event => {

if (event.key === 'Enter') {

channel.push("new_msg", {body: messageInput.value})

messageInput.value = ""

}

})
```

This code does the following:

- Connects to the Phoenix socket at **/socket**.
- Joins the "chat:lobby" channel.
- Listens for "new_msg" events and appends the received messages to the **#chat-box** element in the HTML.
- Captures user input from the **#message-input** field and sends a "new_msg" event to the channel when the user presses Enter.

Step 4: Create the HTML Template

Finally, let's create a simple HTML template to display the chat interface. You can add this to a relevant template file in your Phoenix application (e.g., **lib/my_app_web/templates/page/index.html.eex**):

HTML

```
<div id="chat-box"></div>

<input type="text" id="message-input" placeholder="Type your message...">
```

This code creates a **div** with the ID "chat-box" to display the messages and an input field with the ID "message-input" for users to type their messages.

Now, if you start your Phoenix server and visit the page with this HTML, you should have a functional chat application. You and other users can join the "chat:lobby" channel and exchange messages in real-time.

This is a basic example, but it demonstrates the core concepts of building real-time features with Phoenix Channels. You can expand upon this foundation to create more complex chat applications with features like private messaging, user presence, and more. So, get creative, experiment with channels, and build engaging real-time experiences for your users!

8.3 Presence Tracking

Let's add some awareness to our real-time applications with presence tracking! Imagine you're in that virtual coffee shop we built earlier. Wouldn't it be cool to see who else is online and having a conversation? That's exactly what presence tracking allows you to do. It's like having a radar that shows you who's present in a particular channel or room.

Why Presence Tracking?

Presence tracking opens up a world of possibilities for real-time applications:

- **Show online users:** Display a list of users who are currently online in a chat room or collaborative tool.
- **User activity:** Indicate when a user is actively typing or viewing a document.
- **Notifications:** Notify users when someone joins or leaves a channel.
- **Personalized experiences:** Tailor the user experience based on who is present.

Phoenix.Presence to the Rescue

Phoenix provides a handy module called **Phoenix.Presence** to simplify presence tracking. It handles the complexities of tracking users across different channels and nodes, making it easy to integrate presence features into your applications.

Implementing Presence Tracking

Let's add presence tracking to our chat application:

1. **Add phoenix_live_view to your dependencies:** Presence tracking requires the phoenix_live_view package. Add it to your **mix.exs** file:

Elixir

```
defp deps do

[

{:phoenix_live_view, "~> 0.18.18"} # Or the latest version

]

end
```

2. **Define a presence tracker:**

Elixir

```
# lib/my_app_web/channels/presence.ex

defmodule MyAppWeb.Presence do

use Phoenix.Presence,

otp_app: :my_app,

pubsub_server: MyApp.PubSub
```

end

This code defines a presence tracker that uses your application's PubSub server to manage presence information.

3. **Track presence in your channel:**

Elixir

```elixir
# lib/my_app_web/channels/chat_channel.ex

defmodule MyAppWeb.ChatChannel do

use Phoenix.Channel

def join("chat:lobby", _params, socket) do

send(self(), :after_join)

{:ok, socket}

end


def handle_in("new_msg", %{"body" => body}, socket) do

broadcast! socket, "new_msg", %{body: body,[1] sender: socket.assigns.user_name}

{:noreply, socket}

end
```

```elixir
def handle_info(:after_join, socket) do

push socket, "presence_state",
MyAppWeb.Presence.list("chat:lobby")

MyAppWeb.Presence.track(socket,
socket.assigns.user_id, %{

user_name: socket.assigns.user_name

})

{:noreply, socket}

end

end
```

We've added a handle_info/2 callback that is triggered after a user joins the channel. It uses MyAppWeb.Presence.track/3 to register the user's presence and MyAppWeb.Presence.list/1 to get the current presence state and send it to the client.

4. Handle presence updates on the client:

JavaScript

```javascript
// assets/js/channels/chat_channel.js

// ... (previous code) ...

channel.on("presence_state", state => {

let presences = []
```

```javascript
for (let key in state) {

let presence = state[key]

presences.push(presence.metas[0].user_name)

}

let presenceList =
document.querySelector("#presence-list")

presenceList.innerHTML = `Online: ${presences.join(",
")}`

})

channel.on("presence_diff", diff => {

// Handle presence changes (joins and leaves)

})
```

This code listens for "presence_state" and "presence_diff" events from the channel. The "presence_state" event provides the initial presence list when the user joins, and the "presence_diff" event provides updates when users join or leave.

5. **Add HTML to display the presence list:**

HTML

```html
<div id="presence-list"></div>

<div id="chat-box"></div>
```

```
<input          type="text"          id="message-input"
placeholder="Type your message...">
```

Now, when users join the chat, they'll see a list of online users, and the list will update in real-time as users come and go.

This is a basic example, but it demonstrates the core concepts of presence tracking with Phoenix Channels. You can build upon this to create more sophisticated presence features, such as showing user activity, sending notifications, and personalizing the user experience. So, add presence tracking to your real-time applications and make them more engaging and interactive!

8.4 Scaling Real-time Features

Alright, let's talk about scaling those awesome real-time features you've built with Phoenix Channels! Imagine your chat application becomes super popular, with thousands of users chatting simultaneously. You'll need to make sure your application can handle the increased traffic and maintain a smooth user experience. This is where scaling comes in. Think of it as upgrading your coffee shop from a cozy corner café to a bustling multi-story establishment with plenty of seating and baristas to handle the crowds.

Why Scale?

Scaling your real-time application is crucial for:

- **Performance:** Maintain fast response times and a smooth user experience even with a large number of users.
- **Reliability:** Ensure your application stays up and running even under heavy load.
- **Cost-efficiency:** Optimize resource usage to avoid unnecessary expenses.

Scaling Strategies

There are several strategies you can use to scale your Phoenix Channels application:

1. Vertical Scaling

This involves increasing the resources of your server (CPU, memory, network bandwidth) to handle more traffic. It's like adding more powerful equipment to your coffee shop, such as a bigger espresso machine or a faster oven.

- **Pros:** Simpler to implement than horizontal scaling.
- **Cons:** Can be expensive and has limits to how much you can scale.

2. Horizontal Scaling

This involves adding more servers to distribute the load. It's like opening multiple branches of your coffee shop in different locations.

- **Pros:** Can handle a large number of users and provides redundancy.
- **Cons:** More complex to implement and requires load balancing.

3. Clustering

Phoenix provides built-in support for clustering with libcluster, allowing you to distribute your application across multiple nodes. This enables you to handle a large number of connections and provides fault tolerance. It's like having a network of coffee shops that can share customers and resources.

- **Implementing Clustering:**
  1. **Add libcluster to your dependencies:**

Elixir

```elixir
# mix.exs

defp deps do

[

{:libcluster, "~> 3.0"}

]

end
```

  2. **Configure libcluster:**

Elixir

```elixir
# config/config.exs

config :libcluster,

topologies: [
```

```
my_app: [

strategy: Cluster.Strategy.Kubernetes.DNS,

config: [

service_name: "my_app" # Replace with your service
name

]

]

]
```

3. **Start your application with clustering:**

Bash

```
iex --sname my_app_node_1 -S mix phx.server

iex --sname my_app_node_2 -S mix phx.server
```

4. Caching

Caching frequently accessed data can significantly reduce the load on your database and improve performance. It's like having a display case with pre-made pastries in your coffee shop, so you don't have to bake them every time someone orders them.

Phoenix provides built-in support for caching with Phoenix.PubSub. You can also use external caching solutions like Redis or Memcached.

5. Database Optimization

Optimizing your database queries and schema can improve the performance of your real-time features. This might involve using indexes, optimizing data structures, or choosing the right database technology for your needs. It's like organizing your kitchen and ingredients efficiently to speed up food preparation.

Scaling Phoenix Channels

Phoenix Channels are designed for scalability, but you might need to consider additional strategies for handling a large number of connections:

- **Channel Sharding:** Distribute channels across multiple processes or nodes to avoid overloading a single process.
- **Presence Optimization:** Optimize presence tracking by using efficient data structures and minimizing updates.
- **Backpressure:** Implement mechanisms to handle situations where the server is receiving more messages than it can process.

By combining these scaling strategies, you can build real-time applications that can handle a massive number of users and provide a smooth and enjoyable experience. So, plan for scalability, optimize your code, and let your real-time applications shine!

Chapter 9: Concurrency and Distribution

We're about to explore the exciting world of concurrency and distribution in Elixir. This is where Elixir truly shines, allowing you to build applications that can handle massive amounts of work simultaneously and spread that work across multiple computers. Think of it like having a team of expert chefs working in parallel, each with their own specialized station, to prepare a grand feast.

9.1 OTP in Depth:

Let's dive deeper into the heart of OTP (Open Telecom Platform)! We've already touched on the basics of OTP, but now we'll explore the intricate workings of supervisors, GenServers, and agents. Think of OTP as a well-coordinated team of chefs working together to create a culinary masterpiece. Each chef has a specific role, and they communicate and collaborate to ensure a flawless dining experience.

Supervisors:

Supervisors are the master chefs of OTP. They oversee the work of other processes (their "children") and ensure that everything runs smoothly. Their primary responsibility is to maintain the stability and reliability of your application. If a child process crashes, the supervisor can restart it, preventing a single failure from bringing down the whole system. It's like having a head chef who can quickly replace a cook if they accidentally burn a dish, ensuring the kitchen keeps running smoothly.

Types of Supervisors

OTP provides different supervisor strategies to handle child process failures:

- one_for_one: If one child process crashes, only that specific process is restarted. This is like replacing a single cook who made a mistake.
- one_for_all: If one child process crashes, all child processes are restarted. This is like a fire alarm going off in the kitchen, requiring everyone to evacuate and then restart their work from scratch.
- rest_for_one: If one child process crashes, all child processes started *after* the crashed process are restarted. This is like a power outage affecting a section of the kitchen, requiring those specific stations to be reset.

Defining a Supervisor

Elixir

```elixir
defmodule MyApp.Supervisor do

use Supervisor

def start_link(opts) do

Supervisor.start_link(__MODULE__, opts, name: __MODULE__)[1]

end
```

```elixir
def init(opts) do

children² = [

{MyApp.Worker1, []},

{MyApp.Worker2, []}

]

Supervisor.init(children, strategy: :one_for_one)

end

end
```

This code defines a supervisor that starts two worker processes, **MyApp.Worker1** and **MyApp.Worker2**, using the :one_for_one strategy.

GenServers:

GenServers (Generic Servers) are the workhorses of OTP. They are stateful processes that can handle messages, perform tasks, and maintain data. Think of them as the expert chefs in our kitchen, each responsible for preparing a specific part of the meal.

Key GenServer Callbacks

- **init/1**: Initializes the GenServer's state when it starts. This is like the chef gathering their ingredients and setting up their workstation.
- **handle_call/3**: Handles synchronous messages, where the sender waits for a reply. This is like a

waiter taking an order from a customer and waiting for the dish to be prepared.

- handle_cast/2: Handles asynchronous messages, where the sender doesn't wait for a reply. This is like the head chef instructing a cook to start preparing a certain dish without waiting for confirmation.
- terminate/2: Cleans up resources when the GenServer terminates. This is like the chef cleaning their workstation at the end of their shift.

Creating a GenServer

Elixir

```elixir
defmodule MyApp.Worker1 do

use GenServer

def start_link(state) do

GenServer.start_link(__MODULE__,     state,     name: __MODULE__)

end

def init(state) do

{:ok, state}

end

def³ handle_call(:get_state, _from, state) do

{:reply, state, state}

end
```

```
def handle_cast(:update_state, new_state), do: {:noreply,
new_state}

end
```

This code defines a simple GenServer that stores and updates a state.

Agents:

Agents are like the sous chefs in our kitchen, assisting the main chefs by holding and managing pieces of state. They provide a simpler interface than GenServers when you only need to store and update data without complex message handling.

Using Agents

Elixir

```
iex> {:ok, agent} = Agent.start_link(fn -> 0 end)

{:ok, #PID<0.100.0>}

iex> Agent.update(agent, fn state -> state + 1 end)

:ok

iex> Agent.get(agent, fn state -> state end)

1
```

This code creates an agent that stores an integer value and updates it using the Agent.update/2 function.

By understanding the roles of supervisors, GenServers, and agents, you can build robust and concurrent applications that can handle complex tasks and maintain high availability. So, embrace the power of OTP, utilize its components effectively, and create Elixir applications that are as efficient and reliable as a well-run kitchen!

9.2 Designing for Concurrency

Let's talk about designing applications for concurrency! Concurrency is like having multiple chefs working together in a kitchen. Each chef focuses on a specific task, and they communicate and coordinate to prepare a delicious meal efficiently. In Elixir, we achieve concurrency through processes, which are like those independent chefs, each with their own workspace and responsibilities.

Thinking Concurrently

Designing for concurrency requires a different mindset than traditional sequential programming. Instead of thinking about code as a series of steps executed one after another, you need to think about how to break down your problem into independent tasks that can be executed concurrently.

Key Considerations for Concurrent Design

Here are some key principles to keep in mind when designing concurrent applications:

1. **Identify Concurrent Tasks:** Analyze your application and identify tasks that can be executed independently. These might be long-running operations, tasks that involve waiting for external resources (like network requests), or tasks that can be parallelized.
2. **Minimize Shared State:** Avoid sharing mutable state between processes as much as possible. Sharing mutable data can lead to race conditions and other concurrency bugs, like two chefs trying to use the same knife at the same time. Instead, use message passing to communicate and coordinate between processes.
3. **Embrace Immutability:** Use immutable data structures whenever possible. Immutability simplifies reasoning about concurrent code because you don't have to worry about data changing unexpectedly. It's like each chef having their own set of ingredients that they can't modify, preventing accidental mix-ups.
4. **Handle Errors Gracefully:** Things can go wrong in concurrent systems, just like in a busy kitchen. A chef might drop a dish or run out of an ingredient. Use supervisors to handle process crashes and ensure that your application can recover from failures gracefully.

Example: Concurrent Image Processing

Let's say you're building an application that processes images. You can design it concurrently by:

1. **Identifying Concurrent Tasks:** Each image can be processed independently, making it a good candidate for concurrency.
2. **Creating Worker Processes:** Spawn a process for each image to handle the processing.
3. **Sending Messages:** Send messages to the worker processes with the image data.
4. **Processing Images:** Each worker process receives the image data, performs the processing, and sends the result back to the main process.
5. **Supervising Workers:** Use a supervisor to monitor the worker processes and restart them if they crash.

Code Example (Simplified)

Elixir

```elixir
defmodule MyApp.ImageProcessor do

use GenServer

def start_link() do

GenServer.start_link(__MODULE__,      [],      name:
__MODULE__)

end

def process_image(image_data) do

GenServer.cast(__MODULE__,                {:process_image,
image_data})

end

# ... GenServer callbacks ...
```

```
def handle_cast({:process_image, image_data}, state) do

# ... process the image ...

{:noreply, state}

end

end

# In your main process

{:ok, pid} = MyApp.ImageProcessor.start_link()

MyApp.ImageProcessor.process_image(image_data1)

MyApp.ImageProcessor.process_image(image_data2)
```

This code defines an ImageProcessor GenServer that can process images concurrently. The main process sends messages to the GenServer with the image data, and the GenServer handles the processing in separate processes.

Benefits of Concurrent Design

- **Improved Performance:** Concurrent applications can often perform tasks faster by utilizing multiple cores and processing data in parallel.
- **Increased Responsiveness:** Concurrent applications can handle multiple requests simultaneously, improving responsiveness and user experience.
- **Enhanced Reliability:** Supervisors and process isolation help create fault-tolerant systems that can recover from errors gracefully.

By understanding these principles and applying them to your Elixir applications, you can harness the power of concurrency to build efficient, responsive, and reliable systems. So, think concurrently, embrace immutability, and let your Elixir applications handle multiple tasks with ease!

9.3 Tasks and Processes

Let's talk about the dynamic duo of concurrency in Elixir: tasks and processes! Think of them as two specialized chefs in your kitchen, each with their own unique skills and strengths. Tasks are like the quick and nimble sous chefs, perfect for handling small, focused tasks. Processes, on the other hand, are like the experienced head chefs, capable of managing complex, long-running operations.

Tasks: Lightweight and Efficient

Tasks are lightweight units of execution that run within the same process. They are ideal for short-lived, CPU-bound operations, such as performing calculations, processing data, or making API calls. Think of them as small, focused tasks that can be completed quickly, like chopping vegetables or whisking a sauce.

Creating Tasks

You can create a task using the Task.async/1 function:

Elixir

```
task = Task.async(fn ->
```

164

```
# ... perform some work ...

end)
```

This code creates a task that executes the given anonymous function concurrently.

Getting Results

You can get the result of a task using **Task.await/2**:

Elixir

```
result = Task.await(task, 10000) # Wait up to 10 seconds for the result
```

Processes: Robust and Independent

Processes are independent units of execution with their own memory space. They are ideal for long-lived tasks, I/O-bound operations (like interacting with files or networks), and isolating failures. Think of them as the main chefs responsible for preparing entire dishes or managing specific sections of the kitchen.

Creating Processes

You can create a process using the spawn/1 function:

Elixir

```
pid = spawn(fn ->

# ... perform some work ...
```

end)

This code creates a process that executes the given anonymous function concurrently.

Sending Messages

You can communicate with processes using message passing:

Elixir

```
send(pid, {:message, data})
```

Receiving Messages

Processes can receive messages using the `receive/1` block:

Elixir

```
receive do

{:message, data} -> # ... handle the message ...

end
```

Choosing the Right Tool

When deciding between tasks and processes, consider the following:

- **Task Duration:** Use tasks for short-lived operations and processes for long-lived operations.

- **CPU vs. I/O:** Use tasks for CPU-bound operations and processes for I/O-bound operations.
- **Fault Tolerance:** Use processes for fault isolation, as a crash in one process won't affect others.
- **Complexity:** Tasks are generally simpler to use for basic concurrency, while processes provide more control and features for complex scenarios.

Example: Concurrent Download and Processing

Let's say you need to download multiple files and process them. You can use a combination of tasks and processes:

1. **Download with Tasks:** Create a task for each file download, as downloading is typically an I/O-bound operation.
2. **Process with Processes:** Create a process for each file processing, as processing might be CPU-bound and long-running.
3. **Coordinate with Messages:** Use messages to send the downloaded file data from the tasks to the processes for processing.

Code Example (Simplified)

Elixir

```
# Download task

download_task = Task.async(fn ->

# ... download the file ...

end)

# Processing process
```

```
pid = spawn(fn ->

receive do

{:file_data, data} -> # ... process the data ...

end

end)

# Send file data to the process

file_data = Task.await(download_task)

send(pid, {:file_data, file_data})
```

By understanding the strengths of tasks and processes, you can choose the right tool for the job and build concurrent Elixir applications that are efficient, robust, and maintainable. So, analyze your tasks, consider their characteristics, and let tasks and processes be your partners in concurrency!

9.4 Distributed Elixir with libcluster

Let's explore the exciting world of distributed Elixir with libcluster! Imagine you've outgrown your single kitchen and now have a network of kitchens working together to cater to a massive banquet. That's the power of distribution in Elixir. It allows you to spread your application across multiple machines, forming a cluster that can handle more traffic, increase fault tolerance, and even run geographically distributed applications.

Distributing your Elixir application offers several benefits:

- **Scalability:** Handle more traffic and users by distributing the load across multiple machines. It's like having multiple kitchens to prepare food for a large number of guests.
- **Fault Tolerance:** If one machine fails, the other machines in the cluster can continue operating, ensuring high availability. This is like having backup kitchens ready to take over if one kitchen experiences a problem.
- **Geographic Distribution:** Place nodes closer to your users to reduce latency and improve performance. This is like having kitchens in different cities to serve local customers more efficiently.

libcluster:

libcluster is a powerful library that simplifies the process of creating and managing Elixir clusters. It provides various strategies for node discovery, failure detection, and communication. Think of it as the manager who coordinates the work between different kitchens, ensuring smooth collaboration and efficient resource utilization.

Implementing Distribution with libcluster

Let's see how to distribute your Elixir application with libcluster:

1. **Add libcluster to your dependencies:**

Elixir

```elixir
# mix.exs

defp deps do

[

{:libcluster, "~> 4.0"} # Or the latest version

]

end
```

2. **Configure libcluster:**

```elixir
# config/config.exs

config :libcluster,

topologies: [

my_app: [

strategy: Cluster.Strategy.Kubernetes.DNS, # Or another strategy

config: [

service_name: "my_app" # Replace with your service name

]

]

]
```

This configuration defines a topology named **my_app** and uses the `Cluster.Strategy.Kubernetes.DNS` strategy for node discovery. You can choose a different strategy based on your deployment environment (e.g., `Cluster.Strategy.DNS` for basic DNS-based discovery).

3. **Start your application with clustering:**

Bash

```
iex --sname my_app_node_1 -S mix phx.server

iex --sname my_app_node_2 -S mix phx.server
```

This starts two nodes of your application with different names (**my_app_node_1** and **my_app_node_2**). `libcluster` will automatically discover and connect these nodes, forming a cluster.

Node Discovery Strategies

`libcluster` provides various strategies for nodes to discover each other:

- **DNS:** Uses DNS records to find other nodes.
- **Kubernetes:** Discovers nodes running in a Kubernetes cluster.
- **AWS EC2:** Discovers nodes running on AWS EC2.
- **Multicast:** Uses multicast networking to discover nodes on the same local network.

Distributing Data and Tasks

Once you have a cluster, you can distribute data and tasks across the nodes.

- **Distributed Databases:** Use a distributed database like Riak, Cassandra, or CouchDB to store and access data across the cluster.
- **:global Process Registry:** Use the :global process registry to register processes and access them from any node in the cluster.
- **Distributed Tasks:** Use Task.Supervisor to distribute tasks across the cluster and process them concurrently on different nodes.

Example: Distributed Cache

You can use libcluster and :global to create a simple distributed cache:

Elixir

```elixir
# lib/my_app/cache.ex

defmodule MyApp.Cache do

def put(key, value) do

:global.register_name({:cache, key}, value)

end

def get(key) do

:global.whereis_name({:cache, key})

end

end
```

This code defines a **Cache** module that uses :**global** to store and retrieve cached values. Since :**global** is distributed, the cache will be accessible from any node in the cluster.

By understanding how to use **libcluster** and distribute your Elixir applications, you can build scalable, fault-tolerant, and geographically distributed systems. So, embrace the power of distribution, explore different strategies, and create Elixir applications that can handle the demands of a global audience!

Chapter 10: Debugging and Performance Tuning

Time to put on our detective hats and learn how to find and fix those pesky bugs that inevitably creep into our code! Debugging is a crucial skill for any developer, and Elixir provides a range of tools and techniques to help you track down and eliminate errors. We'll also explore how to make your Elixir applications run faster and more efficiently with performance tuning techniques. Think of this chapter as your guide to becoming an Elixir detective and performance optimizer!

10.1 Debugging Techniques in Elixir

Let's turn into code detectives and learn how to track down and squash those pesky bugs that can sneak into our Elixir programs! Debugging is a crucial skill for any developer, and Elixir provides a range of powerful tools and techniques to help you in your quest to write clean, bug-free code. Think of debugging as a treasure hunt, where you follow clues and use your problem-solving skills to uncover the hidden treasure (or in this case, the source of the bug).

1. IEx:

IEx (Interactive Elixir) is your best friend when it comes to debugging. It's like a playground where you can experiment with code, inspect variables, and pry into the inner workings of your functions.

- **Inspecting Variables:** Use the i/1 function to get detailed information about a variable.

Elixir

iex> my_list = [1, 2, 3]

[1, 2, 3]

iex> i(my_list)

Term

[1, 2, 3]

Data type

List

Reference modules

List

Implemented protocols

Collectable, Enumerable, IEx.Info, Inspect, List.Chars,[1] Sequence

- **Setting Breakpoints with IEx.pry/0:** Insert IEx.pry() in your code to set a breakpoint. When the execution reaches that point, it will pause, and you'll be dropped into an IEx shell within the context of your code. From there, you can inspect variables, call functions, and even modify the state of your program.

Elixir

```
defmodule MyModule do

def my_function(x) do

# ... some code ...

require IEx; IEx.pry()

# ... more code ...

end

end
```

- **Experimenting with Code:** IEx allows you to try out different code snippets and see their results immediately, making it a great tool for understanding how your code behaves and identifying potential issues.

2. IO.inspect/2: Your Trusty Print Statement

The IO.inspect/2 function is like your trusty print statement on steroids. It allows you to print the value of a variable or expression to the console, along with an optional label. This can be incredibly helpful for tracing the flow of data and identifying unexpected values.

Elixir

```
defmodule MyModule do

def my_function(x) do

IO.inspect(x, label: "Value of x:")

# ... some code ...
```

end

end

3. The dbg Macro (Elixir 1.14+): Your Debugging Sidekick

The dbg macro is a powerful new addition to Elixir's debugging toolkit. It provides a concise way to inspect values and even step through your code.

Elixir

```elixir
defmodule MyModule do

def my_function(x, y) do

dbg(x)

dbg(x + y, label: "Result:")

# ... some code ...

end

end
```

dbg will print the value of the given expression along with file and line number information. In some environments (like when running tests with mix test), it even allows you to step through the code execution.

4. Stack Traces: Following the Trail

When an error occurs, Elixir provides a stack trace, which is like a map showing you the path the code took to reach the error. The stack trace lists the sequence of function calls that led to the error, helping you pinpoint the exact location of the problem.

5. Error Logging: Keeping a Record

Use Elixir's logging mechanisms (like the Logger module) to record errors and other relevant information. This can help you identify patterns and track down intermittent issues that might be difficult to reproduce.

6. Testing: Your Bug Prevention Squad

Writing comprehensive tests with ExUnit is one of the best ways to prevent bugs in the first place. Tests act as a safety net, ensuring that your code behaves as expected and catching regressions before they reach production.

Debugging Strategies

- **Reproduce the bug:** The first step is to reliably reproduce the bug. This helps you understand the conditions under which it occurs.
- **Isolate the problem:** Try to narrow down the scope of the problem to a specific function or module.
- **Gather information:** Use the tools and techniques described above to inspect variables, trace code execution, and gather information about the program's state.
- **Form a hypothesis:** Based on the information you've gathered, form a hypothesis about the cause of the bug.
- **Test your hypothesis:** Modify the code to test your hypothesis and see if it resolves the bug.

- **Repeat:** If the bug persists, gather more information, refine your hypothesis, and repeat the process.

By mastering these debugging techniques and applying them strategically, you can effectively track down and eliminate bugs in your Elixir code. So, embrace your inner code detective, utilize these tools, and let your Elixir programs be bug-free and shine!

10.2 The Observer:

Alright, let's get a bird's-eye view of your Elixir system with the Observer! Imagine you have a complex machine with many moving parts, and you want to see how those parts interact and identify any potential issues. The Observer is like an X-ray vision into your Elixir application, providing a graphical interface to visualize processes, their states, and resource usage.

The Observer is a valuable tool for:

- **Understanding your system:** Get a clear picture of how your application is structured and how processes interact.
- **Monitoring performance:** Track CPU and memory usage to identify potential bottlenecks.
- **Debugging:** Inspect the state of processes and identify issues like deadlocks or runaway processes.
- **Troubleshooting:** Diagnose problems and understand the behavior of your application in real-time.

Launching the Observer

You can start the Observer from IEx using the following command:

Elixir

```
iex> :observer.start()
```

This will open a new window with the Observer interface.

Exploring the Observer

The Observer window has several tabs that provide different views of your system:

- **Applications:** This tab shows the running applications and their supervision trees. You can see how processes are organized and supervised, and you can even start, stop, or restart applications from here.
- **Processes:** This tab displays a list of all running processes, their PIDs, registered names, states, and memory usage. You can inspect individual processes to see their details and even send messages to them.
- **Process Info:** When you select a process in the "Processes" tab, this tab shows detailed information about that process, including its state, message queue, and stack trace.
- **ETS Tables:** This tab shows ETS (Erlang Term Storage) tables, which are in-memory data stores used by Elixir processes. You can inspect the contents of these tables and see how they are being used.
- **Load Charts:** This tab displays real-time charts of CPU and memory usage, helping you monitor the

performance of your system and identify potential bottlenecks.

Practical Uses of the Observer

- **Identifying Bottlenecks:** If your application is running slowly, you can use the "Load Charts" tab to see if the CPU or memory is being overutilized. You can then use the "Processes" tab to identify which processes are consuming the most resources.
- **Debugging Deadlocks:** If your application seems stuck, you can use the "Processes" tab to see if any processes are blocked or waiting for each other. This can help you identify deadlocks or other concurrency issues.
- **Inspecting Process State:** If you're debugging a specific process, you can use the "Process Info" tab to inspect its state, message queue, and stack trace. This can help you understand what the process is doing and why it might be behaving unexpectedly.
- **Monitoring Applications:** You can use the "Applications" tab to monitor the health of your applications and their supervised processes. You can also start, stop, or restart applications from this tab.

Tips for Using the Observer

- **Familiarize yourself with the interface:** Spend some time exploring the different tabs and features of the Observer to understand its capabilities.
- **Use filters:** The "Processes" tab has filters that allow you to narrow down the list of processes based on

various criteria, such as process state or registered name.

- **Monitor in real-time:** The Observer provides real-time updates, allowing you to see how your system is behaving as it runs.
- **Combine with other debugging tools:** Use the Observer in conjunction with other debugging tools, such as IEx and IO.inspect, for a more comprehensive debugging experience.

The Observer is a powerful tool for visualizing and understanding your Elixir system. By mastering its features, you can gain valuable insights into the behavior of your applications, identify performance bottlenecks, and debug issues effectively. So, open up the Observer, explore your system, and let it be your guide in building robust and efficient Elixir applications!

10.3 Profiling and Benchmarking

Let's shift gears and talk about performance! Writing code that works correctly is important, but writing code that's also fast and efficient is equally crucial. This is where profiling and benchmarking come in. Think of profiling as using a stopwatch to measure how long each chef in your kitchen takes to prepare their dishes. Benchmarking, on the other hand, is like comparing different recipes to see which one produces the tastiest dish in the shortest amount of time.

Profiling:

Profiling helps you identify which parts of your code are consuming the most time or resources. It's like shining a spotlight on the slowest parts of your application so you can focus your optimization efforts where they'll have the biggest impact.

Elixir's Built-in Profiling Tools

Elixir provides several built-in profiling tools:

- **cprof**: This tool measures the frequency of function calls. It tells you which functions are called most often, which can be a good indicator of where your program is spending most of its time.

Elixir

```
iex> :cprof.start()

:ok

iex> # ... run your code ...

iex> :cprof.stop()

:ok

iex> :cprof.analyse()
```

- **eprof**: This tool measures the time spent in each function. It gives you a more precise view of which functions are taking the longest to execute.

Elixir

iex> :eprof.start()

:ok

iex> # ... run your code ...

iex> :eprof.stop()

:ok

iex> :eprof.analyze()

- **fprof:** This is a more advanced profiling tool that provides detailed information about function calls, timing, and call graphs. It can help you identify performance hotspots and understand the flow of execution in your program.

Elixir

iex> :fprof.trace(:start)

:ok

iex> # ... run your code ...

iex> :fprof.trace(:stop)

:ok

iex> :fprof.profile()

Benchmarking: Comparing Performance

Benchmarking allows you to compare the performance of different code implementations or algorithms. It's like conducting a head-to-head competition between different approaches to see which one comes out on top.

Benchee: Your Benchmarking Buddy

Benchee is a popular Elixir library for benchmarking code. It provides a simple and convenient way to compare the performance of different code snippets and generate reports.

Elixir

```elixir
# Add Benchee to your dependencies:

#  {:benchee, "~> 1.0", only: [:dev, :test]}

defmodule MyBenchmark do

use Benchee

def run do

job = %{

"map/2" => fn -> Enum.map(1..1000, &(&1 * 2)) end,

"for/1" => fn -> for i <- 1..1000, do: i * 2 end

}

Benchee.run(job)
```

end

end

This code benchmarks two different ways to double the numbers from 1 to 1000 using **Enum.map/2** and a `for` comprehension. Benchee will run each function multiple times and provide statistics on their execution time, memory usage, and other metrics.

Interpreting Results

When analyzing profiling and benchmarking results, look for:

- **Hotspots:** Functions or code sections that consume a significant amount of time or resources.
- **Unexpected behavior:** Code that takes longer or uses more resources than expected.
- **Comparison:** Differences in performance between different implementations.

Tips for Profiling and Benchmarking

- **Focus on relevant code:** Profile and benchmark the parts of your code that are most critical for performance.
- **Use realistic data:** Use data that reflects the real-world usage of your application.
- **Run multiple iterations:** Run your benchmarks multiple times to get more reliable results.
- **Consider different scenarios:** Benchmark your code under different conditions, such as varying input sizes or concurrent loads.

By combining profiling and benchmarking, you can gain valuable insights into the performance of your Elixir code and identify areas for optimization. So, grab your stopwatch, run those benchmarks, and let your Elixir code run faster than ever!

10.4 Optimizing Elixir Code

Let's put on our chef hats and learn how to optimize our Elixir code for maximum performance! Just like a chef strives to create the most delicious dishes with the finest ingredients and techniques, we want our Elixir code to be lean, efficient, and performant. Optimizing your code is like fine-tuning a high-performance engine, ensuring that it runs smoothly and efficiently.

Optimizing your Elixir code offers several benefits:

- **Improved performance:** Faster execution, reduced latency, and increased throughput.
- **Reduced resource usage:** Lower memory consumption and CPU utilization.
- **Enhanced scalability:** Handle more users and requests with the same resources.
- **Better user experience:** Provide a smoother and more responsive experience for your users.

Optimization Techniques

Here are some common techniques for optimizing Elixir code:

1. Algorithm Optimization

Choosing the right algorithm and data structure for the task can significantly impact performance. It's like selecting the best recipe and ingredients for a dish.

- **Example:** If you need to search for an element in a list, using Enum.member?/2 is generally faster than iterating through the list manually.

2. Code Refactoring

Refactoring your code to improve its clarity, reduce complexity, and eliminate redundancy can often lead to performance gains. It's like reorganizing your kitchen to make it more efficient and easier to work in.

- **Example:** Extract common code into functions to avoid repetition and improve readability.

3. Database Optimization

Optimizing database queries and schema can significantly improve the performance of your application, especially if it involves frequent database interactions. It's like organizing your pantry and ingredients to quickly find what you need.

- **Example:** Use indexes to speed up database lookups and avoid unnecessary data retrieval.

4. Caching

Caching frequently accessed data can reduce the load on your database and other resources, leading to faster response times. It's like keeping frequently used ingredients readily available on your countertop.

- **Example:** Use **Phoenix.PubSub** or external caching solutions like Redis to cache data that doesn't change frequently.

5. Concurrency

Utilizing concurrency can improve performance by parallelizing tasks and making efficient use of multiple cores. It's like having multiple chefs working simultaneously to prepare a meal faster.

- **Example:** Use tasks or processes to perform independent operations concurrently, such as processing multiple images or making multiple API calls.

6. Tail Recursion

When using recursion, ensure that your functions are tail-recursive to avoid stack overflow errors and improve performance. It's like ensuring that your chefs have a clear and efficient workflow to avoid getting overwhelmed.

7. Reduce Function Calls

Minimize the number of function calls, especially within loops or frequently executed code paths. It's like reducing the number of steps a chef needs to take to prepare a dish.

8. Use the Right Data Structures

Choose the most appropriate data structure for the task. For example, use maps for key-value lookups and sets for efficient membership checks. It's like using the right container to store your ingredients.

9. Avoid Unnecessary Data Copying

Minimize unnecessary data copying, especially when working with large data structures. It's like avoiding unnecessary movement of ingredients in your kitchen.

10. Profile and Benchmark

Use profiling tools (like **cprof**, **eprof**, **fprof**) and benchmarking libraries (like Benchee) to identify performance bottlenecks and measure the impact of your optimizations.

Example: Optimizing a List Operation

Let's say you have a function that filters a list of numbers and then doubles the remaining numbers:

Elixir

```elixir
def double_even_numbers(numbers) do

Enum.filter(numbers, fn x -> rem(x, 2) == 0 end)

|> Enum.map(fn x -> x * 2 end)

end
```

You can optimize this code by combining the filtering and mapping into a single **Enum.reduce/3** operation:

Elixir

```elixir
def double_even_numbers(numbers) do

Enum.reduce(numbers, [], fn x, acc ->
```

```
if rem(x, 2) == 0 do

[x * 2 | acc]

else

 acc

end

end)

|> Enum.reverse()

end
```

This optimized version avoids creating an intermediate list and reduces the number of function calls, potentially improving performance.

By applying these optimization techniques and continuously profiling and benchmarking your code, you can create Elixir applications that are not only functional but also performant and efficient. So, put on your optimization hat, analyze your code, and let your Elixir applications run like a well-oiled machine!

Chapter 11: Microservices with Elixir

Let's explore the world of microservices with Elixir! Imagine instead of one giant kitchen, you have a network of smaller, specialized kitchens working together to prepare a diverse menu. That's the idea behind microservices – breaking down a large application into smaller, independent services that communicate with each other. This approach offers flexibility, scalability, and resilience, making it a popular choice for modern applications.

11.1 Designing Microservices Architectures

Alright, let's dive into the world of microservices architecture! Think of it like building with LEGOs. Instead of one giant, monolithic LEGO castle, you create smaller, independent modules that connect to form a larger structure. Each module has a specific function, like a tower, a drawbridge, or a gatehouse. This is the essence of microservices – breaking down a large application into smaller, self-contained services that work together.

Microservices offer a more flexible and scalable approach to building applications compared to traditional monolithic architectures. Here's why:

- **Agility:** Each service can be developed, deployed, and scaled independently. This allows teams to work on different parts of the application without stepping on each other's toes. It's like having separate construction crews working on different modules of your LEGO castle simultaneously.

- **Scalability:** You can scale specific services based on their individual needs. If your user authentication service is experiencing high traffic, you can scale it up without affecting other parts of the application. This is like adding more bricks to reinforce a specific tower in your LEGO castle.
- **Resilience:** If one service fails, it doesn't necessarily bring down the entire application. Other services can continue operating, providing a more robust and fault-tolerant system. This is like having one tower collapse in your LEGO castle without affecting the rest of the structure.
- **Technology Diversity:** You can use different technologies for different services based on their specific requirements. One service might be best suited for Elixir, while another might benefit from using a different language or framework. This is like using different types of LEGO bricks to create different parts of your castle.
- **Team Autonomy:** Smaller teams can own and manage individual services, promoting greater autonomy and responsibility. This is like assigning different construction crews to different modules of your LEGO castle.

Key Considerations for Microservice Design

Designing a microservices architecture requires careful consideration of several factors:

1. **Decomposition:** How do you break down your application into smaller services? Identify business capabilities or domains that can be separated into independent units. Each service should have a well-defined responsibility and clear boundaries. This is like deciding which modules to create for your LEGO castle – a gatehouse, a keep, a stable, etc.
2. **Communication:** How will your services communicate with each other? Common approaches include:
   - **Synchronous communication:** Services communicate directly with each other using protocols like REST or gRPC. This is like having phone calls between different construction crews.
   - **Asynchronous communication:** Services communicate indirectly through message queues or event streams. This is like leaving messages on a shared whiteboard for other crews to pick up.
3. **Data Management:** Each service should own its data and be responsible for its persistence. This promotes loose coupling and allows services to evolve independently. This is like each construction crew having its own set of instructions and materials for their module.
4. **Deployment:** How will you deploy and manage your services? Consider using containers (Docker), orchestration platforms (Kubernetes), or serverless functions. This is like deciding how to transport and assemble your LEGO modules to build the complete castle.

5. **Monitoring and Observability:** How will you monitor the health and performance of your services? Implement logging, tracing, and metrics to gain insights into your system. This is like having supervisors inspect each module of your LEGO castle to ensure its stability and quality.

Example: E-commerce Application

Let's imagine you're building an e-commerce application. You could decompose it into the following microservices:

- **Product Catalog Service:** Manages product information, including names, descriptions, and prices.
- **Inventory Service:** Tracks product availability and stock levels.
- **Order Service:** Handles order creation, payment processing, and fulfillment.
- **User Service:** Manages user accounts and authentication.
- **Recommendation Service:** Provides personalized product recommendations.

These services could communicate using a combination of synchronous and asynchronous communication, depending on their needs. For example, the Order Service might use synchronous communication to check product availability with the Inventory Service, while the Recommendation Service might use asynchronous communication to update user profiles based on their browsing history.

Code Example (Conceptual)

While a complete code example would be extensive, here's a conceptual example of how you might define a service in Elixir:

Elixir

```elixir
defmodule MyApp.ProductService do

use GenServer

# ... functions for managing product data ...

def get_product(product_id) do

# ... fetch product data from the database ...

end

def update_product(product_id, attrs) do

# ... update product data in the database ...

end

end
```

This code defines a **ProductService** GenServer that encapsulates the logic for managing product data. Other services could interact with this service using message passing or gRPC calls.

By carefully considering these design principles and applying them to your Elixir applications, you can leverage the power of microservices to build flexible, scalable, and resilient systems. So, embrace the LEGO approach, break down your application into manageable services, and let your Elixir microservices work together harmoniously!

11.2 Inter-service Communication with gRPC

Let's explore how to connect those microservices and enable them to communicate with each other using gRPC! Think of gRPC as a modern, high-speed communication system for your microservices, like a network of fiber optic cables transmitting data quickly and reliably. It's a powerful alternative to traditional REST APIs, offering performance, efficiency, and type safety.

Why gRPC?

gRPC (Google Remote Procedure Call) is a modern, open-source framework for inter-service communication. It offers several advantages over REST APIs:

- **Performance:** gRPC uses Protocol Buffers (protobuf), a binary serialization format, which is more compact and efficient than JSON or XML used in REST APIs. It also leverages HTTP/2, which provides features like multiplexing and header compression for faster communication.
- **Type Safety:** Protobuf enforces type checking, ensuring that the data exchanged between services is consistent and valid. This helps prevent errors and improves data integrity.

- **Streaming:** gRPC supports bi-directional streaming, allowing services to send and receive streams of data in real-time. This is useful for applications that require continuous data flow, such as video streaming or real-time analytics.

Implementing gRPC in Elixir

Let's see how to implement gRPC communication between two Elixir microservices:

Step 1: Define the Service with Protobuf

First, we need to define the interface for our gRPC service using Protocol Buffers (protobuf). Protobuf is a language-agnostic way to describe the structure of data and the methods that services can call.

Create a .proto file (e.g., user_service.proto) and define your service:

Protocol Buffers

```
syntax = "proto3";

package my_app;

service UserService {

rpc GetUser (GetUserRequest) returns (UserResponse) {}

}

message GetUserRequest {

  string user_id = 1;
```

}

message UserResponse {

string **name** = 1;

string **email** = 2;

}

This code defines a service called UserService with a single method GetUser. The method takes a GetUserRequest message (containing a user_id) and returns a UserResponse message (containing the user's name and email).

Step 2: Generate Elixir Code

Next, we need to generate Elixir code from our protobuf definition. We'll use the protoc compiler with the Elixir gRPC plugin.

Bash

```
protoc         --proto_path=.           --grpc-gen_out=.
--plugin=protoc-gen-grpc=`which    grpc_elixir_plugin`
user_service.proto
```

This command generates two files: user_service.pb.ex (containing the protobuf message definitions) and user_service_pb_grpc.ex (containing the gRPC service definition).

Step 3: Implement the gRPC Server

Now, let's implement the gRPC server in one of our microservices:

Elixir

```
# lib/my_app/user_server.ex

defmodule MyApp.UserServer do

use GRPC.Server, protoc_gen_elixir_version: "0.11.0" #
Or latest version

def get_user(request, _context) do

user = MyApp.Accounts.get_user(request.user_id)

%UserResponse{name: user.name, email: user.email}

end

end
```

This code defines a **UserServer** module that implements the **get_user** method from our protobuf definition. It fetches the user from the database and returns a **UserResponse** message.

Step 4: Start the gRPC Server

In your application's supervision tree, start the gRPC server:

Elixir

```
# lib/my_app/application.ex

def start(_type, _args) do
```

```elixir
children = [

# ... other processes ...

{GRPC.Server.Supervisor, {MyApp.UserServer, 50051}}

]

Supervisor.start_link(children, strategy: :one_for_one)
end
```

This code starts a gRPC server supervisor that listens on port 50051.

Step 5: Call the gRPC Service from Another Microservice

Finally, let's call the gRPC service from another microservice:

Elixir

```elixir
# lib/my_app/order_service.ex

defmodule MyApp.OrderService do

def create_order(user_id, items) do

{:ok, channel} = GRPC.Channel.new("localhost:50051", [])

stub = MyApp.UserService.Stub.new(channel)

{:ok, response} = stub.get_user(%GetUserRequest{user_id: user_id})
```

```
# ... use the user information to create the order ...

end

end
```

This code creates a gRPC channel to the **UserServer**, creates a stub for the **UserService**, and calls the **get_user** method to retrieve user information.

By following these steps, you can establish efficient and type-safe communication between your Elixir microservices using gRPC. So, define your services, generate the code, start the servers, and let your microservices communicate seamlessly!

11.3 Deploying and Managing Microservices

Let's talk about getting those microservices out into the world! Deploying and managing microservices can be a bit more involved than deploying a monolithic application. Think of it like coordinating the grand opening of multiple restaurants instead of just one. You need to make sure each restaurant has the right location, equipment, staff, and supplies, and that they can all work together smoothly.

Deployment Strategies

There are several strategies for deploying microservices:

1. **Containers (Docker):** Containers are like portable kitchens that package your microservice and its dependencies into a self-contained unit. This ensures

consistency across different environments and simplifies deployment.

- o **Build a Docker image:**

Dockerfile

```
FROM elixir:1.14

WORKDIR /app

COPY mix.exs mix.lock ./

RUN mix deps.get

COPY . .

RUN mix compile

CMD ["mix", "phx.server"]
```

- o **Run the Docker container:**

Bash

```
docker build -t my_app .

docker run -p 4000:4000 my_app
```

2. **Orchestration (Kubernetes):** Orchestration platforms like Kubernetes are like restaurant managers that automate the deployment, scaling, and management of your microservices. They handle tasks like

scheduling containers, managing resources, and monitoring health.

    ○ **Define a Kubernetes deployment:**

YAML

```yaml
apiVersion: apps/v1

kind: Deployment

metadata:

name: my-app

spec:

replicas: 3

selector:

matchLabels:

app: my-app

template:

metadata:

labels:

app: my-app

spec:

containers:
```

- name: my-app

image: my_app:latest[1]

ports:

- containerPort:[2] 4000

   - **Apply the deployment:**

Bash

kubectl apply -f deployment.yaml

3. **Serverless Functions:** Serverless platforms allow you to deploy your microservices as functions that are triggered by events. This can be a cost-effective way to run microservices, as you only pay for the resources you use.

Management Considerations

- **Service Discovery:** How do your services find each other in a dynamic environment? Use service discovery tools like Consul or etcd to register and discover services.
- **API Gateway:** Use an API gateway to provide a single entry point for clients, handle routing, authentication, and rate limiting.
- **Centralized Logging:** Collect logs from all your services in a central location for monitoring and troubleshooting.

- **Monitoring and Alerting:** Monitor the health and performance of your services and set up alerts for critical events.

Deployment Tools

- **Docker:** A platform for building, shipping, and running containerized applications.
- **Kubernetes:** An open-source system for automating deployment, scaling, and management of containerized applications.[3]
- **Fly.io:** A platform for deploying and managing Elixir applications globally, with built-in support for Elixir and Phoenix.
- **Gigalixir:** Another platform specifically designed for deploying Elixir applications, offering features like automatic scaling and database provisioning.

Example: Deploying to Fly.io

1. **Create a** fly.toml **file:**

Ini, TOML

```
app = "my_app"

primary_region = "ams"

[build]

builder = "heroku/buildpacks:20"

[env]

PORT = "4000"
```

```
DATABASE_URL = "postgres://..."  # Your database
connection string
```

```
[deploy]
```

```
release_command = "mix phx.migrate"
```

2. **Deploy the application:**

Bash

```
flyctl launch
```

```
flyctl deploy
```

By understanding these deployment and management considerations and utilizing the available tools, you can effectively deploy and manage your Elixir microservices. So, containerize your services, orchestrate your deployments, and let your microservices run smoothly in the cloud!

Chapter 12: Production-Ready Elixir

We've prepare your awesome Elixir applications for the real world. Deploying to production is like opening your restaurant to the public. You want to ensure everything runs smoothly, customers have a great experience, and you're ready to handle any situation that arises. This chapter covers deployment strategies, release management, monitoring, logging, and essential security practices.

12.1 Deployment Strategies

Let's get your Elixir applications ready for the grand opening! Deploying your application is like setting up your restaurant kitchen for the first time. You need to carefully choose your equipment, arrange your ingredients, and ensure everything is in place for a smooth and successful service. In this section, we'll explore three popular deployment strategies for Elixir applications: Distillery, Docker, and Kubernetes.

1. Distillery:

Distillery is a powerful tool for creating self-contained releases of your Elixir applications. Think of it as packaging your entire kitchen, including the oven, utensils, and ingredients, into a portable container that you can easily transport and set up anywhere.

Why Distillery?

- **Simplicity:** Distillery simplifies the deployment process by bundling everything your application needs into a single package.
- **Efficiency:** Releases created with Distillery are optimized for production, resulting in smaller file sizes and faster startup times.
- **Reliability:** Distillery ensures that your application has all its dependencies and runs consistently across different environments.

Steps to Deploy with Distillery

1. **Add Distillery to your project:**

Bash

```
mix escript.install hex distillery

mix deps.get
```

2. **Initialize Distillery:**

Bash

```
mix release.init
```

This generates a rel directory with configuration files for your release.

3. **Configure your release:**

Edit the **rel/config.exs** file to configure your release. You can specify environment variables, include or exclude files, and customize other settings.

Elixir

rel/config.exs

use **Mix.Releases.Config**, otp_app: :my_app

environment :prod do

  set :environment, :prod

  set :include_erts, true

  set :server, true

  set :runtime_tools, :as_production

end

4. **Build the release:**

Bash

MIX_ENV=prod mix release

This creates a release in the _build/prod/rel/my_app directory.

5. **Deploy the release:**

Copy the release to your server and start it using the provided scripts:

Bash

```
# On your server

_build/prod/rel/my_app/bin/my_app start
```

2. Docker:

Docker allows you to containerize your application, packaging it and its dependencies into a portable image. This ensures consistency across different environments and simplifies deployment. It's like having a blueprint for your kitchen that you can use to create identical copies anywhere.

Why Docker?

- **Portability:** Docker containers can run on any system that has Docker installed, making them highly portable.
- **Consistency:** Docker ensures that your application runs the same way in development, testing, and production.
- **Isolation:** Docker containers isolate your application from the host system, preventing conflicts and dependencies.

Steps to Deploy with Docker

1. **Create a Dockerfile:**

Dockerfile

```
FROM elixir:1.14

WORKDIR /app

COPY mix.exs mix.lock ./

RUN mix deps.get

COPY . .

RUN mix compile

CMD ["mix", "phx.server"]
```

2. **Build the Docker image:**

Bash

```
docker build -t my_app .
```

3. **Deploy the Docker container:**

You can deploy the Docker container to various platforms, including cloud providers like AWS, Google Cloud, and Azure, or container orchestration platforms like Kubernetes.

3. Kubernetes:

Kubernetes is a powerful platform for automating deployment, scaling, and management of containerized applications. It's like having a sophisticated management system for your restaurant that handles staffing, inventory, and customer flow.

Why Kubernetes?

- **Scalability:** Kubernetes makes it easy to scale your application by adding or removing containers as needed.
- **Resilience:** Kubernetes can automatically restart failed containers and ensure high availability.
- **Self-healing:** Kubernetes can monitor the health of your containers and take corrective actions if necessary.

Steps to Deploy with Kubernetes

1. **Package your application as a Docker image.**
2. **Define your Kubernetes deployment:**

Create YAML files to define your Kubernetes deployment, including the Docker image to use, the number of replicas, and other configurations.

apiVersion: apps/v1 kind: Deployment metadata: name: my-app spec: replicas: 3 selector: matchLabels: app: my-app template: metadata: labels: app: my-app spec: containers: - name: my-app image: my_app:latest[1] ports: - containerPort:[2] 4000

3. Deploy to Kubernetes:

Use the `kubectl` command-line tool to deploy your application to a Kubernetes cluster.

By understanding these deployment strategies and choosing the one that best suits your needs, you can effectively deploy your Elixir applications to production. So, choose your deployment method, package your application, and let your Elixir code shine in the real world!

12.2 Release Management

Let's talk about managing the lifecycle of your Elixir applications in production! Release management is like orchestrating a series of grand openings for your restaurant, each introducing new dishes, improved service, or a revamped ambiance. It's the process of carefully planning, building, deploying, and monitoring new versions of your application to ensure a smooth transition and minimize disruptions for your users.

Why Release Management Matters

Effective release management is crucial for:

- **Minimizing downtime:** Reduce disruptions to your users by deploying new versions with minimal downtime or service interruption.
- **Ensuring quality:** Deliver high-quality releases by incorporating testing and quality assurance processes.
- **Managing risk:** Reduce the risk of introducing bugs or regressions by having a well-defined release process.

- **Facilitating collaboration:** Coordinate the efforts of developers, testers, and operations teams to ensure smooth releases.

Key Aspects of Release Management

1. **Versioning:** Assign unique version numbers to each release of your application. This helps you track changes, identify specific releases, and manage dependencies. Common versioning schemes include semantic versioning (e.g., v1.2.3) or date-based versioning (e.g., 20241201).

2. **Deployment Strategies:** Choose a deployment strategy that minimizes downtime and risk. Here are a few popular options:
   - **Rolling deployments:** Gradually roll out the new version to a subset of servers, monitoring for issues before deploying to the rest. This is like gradually introducing new dishes to your menu, getting feedback before making them widely available.
   - **Blue/green deployments:** Deploy the new version to a separate environment (the "green" environment), test it thoroughly, and then switch traffic from the old environment (the "blue" environment) to the new one. This is like setting up a new kitchen alongside your existing one, testing it out before switching over.
   - **Canary deployments:** Roll out the new version to a small percentage of users, monitor their experience, and gradually increase the rollout if everything looks good. This is like offering a

new dish as a "special" to a few customers before adding it to the main menu.

3. **Rollback:** Have a plan for rolling back to a previous version if issues arise with the new release. This is like having a backup menu in case a new dish proves unpopular or causes problems.

4. **Monitoring:** Monitor your application after deployment to identify any issues or performance regressions. This is like keeping a close eye on your restaurant after introducing new dishes or making changes to the service.

Tools for Release Management

- **Distillery:** Provides tools for building releases, managing upgrades, and rolling back to previous versions.
- **Git:** Use Git for version control and to track changes to your code. Tag specific commits with release versions.
- **CI/CD pipelines:** Automate your build, test, and deployment process using continuous integration and continuous delivery (CI/CD) pipelines. Tools like GitHub Actions, GitLab CI/CD, and CircleCI can help you automate your release workflow.

Example: Release Management with Distillery and Git

1. **Create a release with Distillery:**

Bash

```
MIX_ENV=prod mix release --upgrade
```

The --upgrade flag generates an upgrade task that can be used to upgrade an existing release.

2. **Tag the release in Git:**

Bash

```
git tag v1.2.3

git push --tags
```

3. **Deploy the release to your server:**

Upload the release to your server and run the upgrade task:

Bash

```
# On your server

_build/prod/rel/my_app/bin/my_app upgrade v1.2.3
```

4. **Monitor the release:**

Use monitoring tools to track the health and performance of the new release.

By implementing a robust release management process and utilizing the available tools, you can ensure smooth and reliable deployments of your Elixir applications. So, plan your releases, automate your deployments, and deliver high-quality software with confidence!

12.3 Monitoring and Logging

Let's talk about keeping a watchful eye on your Elixir applications in production! Monitoring and logging are like having a team of observant waiters and a detailed logbook in your restaurant. They help you understand how your application is performing, identify potential issues, and troubleshoot problems when they arise.

Monitoring and logging are essential for:

- **Understanding application behavior:** Gain insights into how your application is being used, identify usage patterns, and track key metrics. This is like observing customer behavior in your restaurant to understand their preferences and optimize the menu.
- **Detecting anomalies:** Identify unusual behavior or performance issues that might indicate problems. This is like noticing a sudden drop in customer orders or an increase in complaints, signaling a potential issue in the kitchen.
- **Troubleshooting problems:** When issues occur, logs provide valuable clues to help you diagnose and resolve them. This is like reviewing the logbook to track down the source of a foodborne illness or a customer complaint.
- **Ensuring uptime and performance:** Monitor critical metrics to ensure your application is running smoothly and meeting performance expectations. This is like keeping an eye on the kitchen's efficiency and ensuring that orders are prepared and delivered on time.

Monitoring Tools

Several tools can help you monitor your Elixir applications:

- **Prometheus:** A popular open-source monitoring system that collects metrics from your application and stores them in a time-series database. It's like having a set of sensors in your restaurant that track various metrics, such as temperature, humidity, and customer traffic.
- **Grafana:** A tool for visualizing data from Prometheus and other sources. It allows you to create dashboards and alerts to monitor your application's performance and health. This is like having a control panel that displays real-time data from your sensors and alerts you to any anomalies.
- **AppSignal:** A commercial monitoring service with excellent Elixir support. It provides detailed performance monitoring, error tracking, and host metrics. This is like having a dedicated team of analysts monitoring your restaurant's performance and providing insights and recommendations.

Implementing Monitoring with Prometheus and Grafana

1. **Add the prometheus.ex dependency:**

Elixir

```
# mix.exs

defp deps do
  [
```

```elixir
{:prometheus.ex, "~> 1.0"}
```

]

end

2. **Configure Prometheus:**

```elixir
# config/config.exs

config :prometheus,

scrape_interval: :timer.seconds(15)
```

3. **Instrument your code:**

```elixir
defmodule MyApp.MyModule do

use Prometheus.Instrumented

# Define a counter metric

counter :my_counter,

help: "Number of times something happened",

tags: [:status]

def my_function(status) do

Prometheus.inc(:my_counter, 1, tags: [status: status])
```

```
# ... your function logic ...

end

end
```

4. **Start the Prometheus endpoint:**

Elixir

```
# lib/my_app/application.ex

def start(_type, _args) do

children = [

# ... other processes ...

Prometheus.Endpoint

]

Supervisor.start_link(children, strategy: :one_for_one)

end
```

5. **Install and configure Grafana:**

Download and install Grafana. Configure it to connect to your Prometheus instance and create dashboards to visualize your metrics.

Logging

Elixir provides the Logger module for logging events and errors in your application.

- **Configure logging:**

Elixir

```
# config/config.exs

config :logger,

backends: [:console, :file],

level: :info
```

- **Log messages:**

Elixir

```
Logger.info("Something happened")

Logger.error("An error occurred")
```

- **Centralized logging:**

  Consider sending your logs to a centralized logging system like Elasticsearch, Logstash, and Kibana (ELK) or Graylog for easier analysis and searching.

By combining monitoring tools with effective logging practices, you can gain valuable insights into your Elixir applications and ensure they are running smoothly in production. So, set up your monitoring system, configure your logging, and keep a watchful eye on your Elixir applications!

12.4 Security Best Practices

Let's fortify your Elixir applications and protect them from potential threats! Security is like having a strong security system in your restaurant – alarms, surveillance cameras, and well-trained staff – to prevent theft, vandalism, and other unwanted incidents. In the digital world, security is equally crucial to protect your application, data, and users from malicious attacks.

Why Security Matters

Security breaches can have severe consequences:

- **Data Loss:** Loss of sensitive data, such as customer information or financial records.
- **Reputation Damage:** Loss of trust and damage to your reputation.
- **Financial Loss:** Costs associated with recovering from an attack and potential legal liabilities.
- **Service Disruption:** Downtime and disruption of services to your users.

Security Best Practices for Elixir Applications

1. **Authentication and Authorization:**
   - **Verify user identity:** Implement robust authentication mechanisms to verify the identity of users accessing your application. Use strong passwords, multi-factor authentication, or OAuth 2.0 for secure authentication.
   - **Control access:** Use authorization mechanisms to control access to different parts of your

application and its data. Implement role-based access control (RBAC) or access control lists (ACLs) to define permissions for different users or groups.

Elixir

```elixir
defmodule MyAppWeb.AuthController do

use MyAppWeb, :controller

def login(conn, %{"email" => email, "password" => password}) do

case MyApp.Accounts.authenticate_user(email, password) do

{:ok, user} ->

conn

|> put_session(:user_id, user.id)

|> redirect(to: "/")

{:error, :invalid_credentials} ->

conn

|> put_flash(:error, "Invalid email or password")

|> render("login.html")

end
```

end

end

2. **Input Validation:**
   - **Sanitize and validate all user input:** Never trust user input! Always sanitize and validate data received from users to prevent injection attacks, such as SQL injection or cross-site scripting (XSS).

Elixir

```elixir
defmodule MyAppWeb.PostController do

use MyAppWeb, :controller

def create(conn, %{"post" => post_params}) do

case MyApp.Blog.create_post(post_params) do

{:ok, post} ->

# ...

{:error, changeset} ->

# Handle validation errors

end

end

end
```

3. **Secure Configuration:**
    - **Protect sensitive data:** Store sensitive data, such as API keys, database credentials, and encryption keys, securely. Use environment variables, configuration management tools, or secrets management services to avoid hardcoding sensitive information in your code.
    - **Secure your endpoints:** Disable any unused endpoints or functionality in your application. Use HTTPS to encrypt communication between your application and its clients.
4. **Dependency Management:**
    - **Keep dependencies up to date:** Regularly update your dependencies to patch security vulnerabilities. Use tools like mix deps.update and sobelow to check for outdated or vulnerable dependencies.
5. **Code Reviews:**
    - **Conduct regular code reviews:** Code reviews can help identify potential security issues and ensure that security best practices are being followed.
6. **Security Audits:**
    - **Perform regular security audits:** Engage security experts to conduct periodic security audits to identify and address vulnerabilities in your application and infrastructure.
7. **Least Privilege Principle:**
    - **Grant only necessary permissions:** Follow the principle of least privilege by granting users and processes only the minimum necessary permissions to perform their tasks.

8. **Defense in Depth:**
    - ○ **Implement multiple layers of security:** Don't rely on a single security mechanism. Implement multiple layers of security, such as firewalls, intrusion detection systems, and security information and event management (SIEM) systems.
9. **Security Training:**
    - ○ **Educate your team:** Provide security training to your development and operations teams to raise awareness of security best practices and common threats.

By incorporating these security best practices into your Elixir development process, you can create applications that are resilient to attacks and protect your valuable data and users. So, be vigilant, stay informed about security threats, and build secure Elixir applications that you and your users can trust!

Conclusion

As we reach the end of this book, I hope you feel a sense of accomplishment and excitement for the possibilities that Elixir unlocks. We've covered a lot of ground, from the foundational principles of functional programming to the intricacies of building robust, concurrent, and distributed applications. You've learned how to wield the power of Elixir and its ecosystem to create applications that are not only functional but also elegant, maintainable, and scalable.

But this is just the beginning of your Elixir journey. The real magic happens when you apply these concepts and techniques to build real-world projects that solve real-world problems. Whether you're crafting high-performance web applications with Phoenix, creating fault-tolerant systems with OTP, or venturing into the world of microservices, Elixir empowers you to build software that can handle the demands of today's ever-evolving digital landscape.

Remember the core principles that make Elixir so compelling:

- **Concurrency:** Embrace the power of lightweight processes and message passing to build applications that can handle massive concurrency with ease.
- **Fault tolerance:** Leverage the "let it crash" philosophy and OTP's supervision trees to create resilient systems that can recover from errors gracefully.
- **Functional programming:** Embrace immutability, pattern matching, and higher-order functions to write clean, concise, and maintainable code.
- **Community and ecosystem:** Tap into the vibrant Elixir community and its rich ecosystem of libraries and frameworks to accelerate your development and find support along the way.

As you continue your Elixir journey, remember to:

- **Stay curious:** Explore new libraries, experiment with different approaches, and keep learning.
- **Embrace the functional mindset:** Think in terms of immutability, data transformations, and composability.
- **Contribute to the community:** Share your knowledge, contribute to open-source projects, and help others learn Elixir.

The future of software development is concurrent, distributed, and increasingly demanding. Elixir, with its elegant syntax, powerful concurrency model, and focus on fault tolerance, is well-equipped to tackle these challenges. So, go forth, build amazing things with Elixir, and be a part of shaping the future of technology.

Happy coding!